Suggestions On The Banks And Currency Of The Several United States, In Reference Principally To The Suspension Of Specie Payments...

Albert Gallatin

SUGGESTIONS

ON THE

BANKS AND CURRENCY

OF

THE SEVERAL UNITED STATES,

IN REFERENCE PRINCIPALLY TO THE

SUSPENSION OF SPECIE PAYMENTS.

BY ALBERT GALLATIN.

NEW-YORK:

WILEY AND PUTNAM.

1841.

Printed by J. P. Wright, 18 New Street, N. Y.

TABLE OF CONTENTS.

PRELIMINARY OBSERVATIONS.

ALL the Banks of the United States are joint stock companies, generally incorporated by the special laws of the several States; in a few late instances established in conformity with the provisions of a general law. In neither case are the shareholders responsible beyond the amount of the capital subscribed. All these joint stock companies are banks of deposit, discount and issue; they all discount negotiable paper, purchase and sell domestic and occasionally foreign bills of exchange, receive deposits, or open cash credits to individuals, and issue bank notes, always, nominally at least, payable on demand in specie (a). These notes have become the local and sole currency of the several places or sections of country where they are respectively made payable. Banking in America always implies the right and the practice of issuing paper money as a substitute for a specie currency.

On the 1st of January 1830 and 1840, respectively, the capital, liabilities payable on demand, and resources, of all the chartered banks in the United States, were, as far as can be ascertained, nearly as follows, viz. :

	1830.	1840.
Number of Banks.................	322	659
Capital $145,000,000		$343,000,000
Actual Circulation and Deposits, payable on demand, 100,000,000		158,000,000
Other liabilities................................... not great		44,000,000
	245,000,000	545,000,000
Discounted Paper, Stocks and Securities, altogether 216,000,000		513,000,000
Specie.. 20,000,000		32,000,000
	236,000,000	545,000,000

(a) Post-notes, not payable on demand, may be sold and purchased, as other negotiable paper, vary in value, and do not form part of the currency proper.

2

There can be no doubt that, in their origin, the Banks were instituted for the purpose of affording accommodations to the commercial interest, and of supplying the want of a capital proportionate to the extent of the legitimate commerce of the country. The prodigious increase of banking capital and accommodations within the last ten years, so much exceeding that which might be actually wanted for promoting the productive industry of the country, has been attended with consequences affecting all classes, and so fatal, in reference to the currency, that it appears proper, in the first place, to ascertain what are the benefits actually bestowed on the community at large by the substitution of a paper for a specie currency: and these advantages must be reduced to their true value, by distinguishing those which belong exclusively to the issues of paper money, from those which might be equally enjoyed with banks and bankers issuing no paper currency and carrying on every other species of banking operations.

These advantages appear to be, commercial punctuality, and the facilities afforded in effecting payments, collecting debts, and making remittances; the conversion of unproductive into productive capital; the saving of a capital tantamount to the enjoyment of an additional capital, and bearing a certain proportion to the amount of paper issues. All but the last might be equally attained with banks or private bankers who issued no paper currency.

Punctuality in fulfilling engagements should be practised by all; but it is essentially a commercial virtue. Credit, at least to a certain extent, is absolutely necessary to commerce. Every merchant must, for the fulfilment of his own engagements, depend principally on the punctual payment of the debts due to him. This punctuality is so necessary, and the advantages derived from it have become so habitual, that the memory of its origin may be lost. It was indubitably due to the establishment of banks. At the close of the war of Independence, Philadelphia was the only place in the United States where commercial punctuality was general, and that city was indebted for it to the Bank of North America. The same effect was successively produced, as banks were established, in New-York, Boston, Baltimore, and the other commercial cities; and finally almost universally, or wherever country banking has penetrated.

It must be observed, that a very small banking capital was sufficient for that purpose, since that object was attained, in each of the several commercial cities, by a single bank, with a capital of not more than five to eight hundred thousand dollars. The merchant who did not pay his discounted note could no longer receive accommodations from the bank ; and .the protest of a note, either discounted or placed in the bank for collection, became soon sufficient to prostrate his credit. But the result would have been the same, had the bank been only one of deposit and discount, and not of issue. Commercial punctuality is as indispensable and universal in all the cities of continental Europe as in America, though no banks of issue existed there, except in Amsterdam, in Paris, and very lately in some other towns of France. This great advantage, though it had its origin here in banks of issue, is not one which belongs exclusively to such banks.

The same observation will apply to the conversion of unproductive into productive capital, which has been effected by our banks. Every merchant, every person, who enjoys or earns a certain income, always keeps on hand a certain amount of currency proportionate to his engagements, to his wealth, and to his wants. So long as it remains in his possession, it is altogether unproductive. Deposited in bank, it becomes a part of the funds applied by the banks to discounts, or in other words, to advances made to the commerce, manufactures, and generally to the productive industry of the country. But, in order to produce that effect, it is sufficient that the bank should be one of deposit, and not that it should issue bank notes. Throughout Europe, the same description of persons who here make deposits, or, which is the same thing, who keep an account with our banks of issue, do deposit or keep an account with private bankers who issue no bank notes. And those bankers give the same facilities in effecting payments, collecting debts, and making remittances, which are afforded by the American banks of issue.

It is therefore principally, if not exclusively, in the substitution of a paper currency, which costs little or nothing, for one in gold and silver, which has an intrinsic value, that the benefit derived from the paper issues does consist. The actual circulation of all the banks in the United States does not, when in a healthy situation, much exceed eighty millions of dollars. Deducting twenty millions in specie, which the banks must keep, on an average, to meet demands on that part of their liabilities, there remain sixty millions, which, instead of being applied to the purchase of gold and silver currency, are applied to productive purposes, and add as much to the productive capital of the country. It may already be inferred that the deposits must not be included in the computation, and that the profit consists only of the difference between the actual issues and the specie kept to meet demands on that account: but this branch of the subject requires further explanation.

The exchange of the commodities produced in different countries, or in different districts of the same country, is the basis of all the commercial transactions between those countries or districts. As that commerce becomes more extensive and regular, the principle of the division of labor is applied; the purchase and importation of the foreign, and the exportation and sale of the domestic commodities given in exchange, become distinct branches of business; masses of respective credits and debits are created; and by far the greater part of the actual payments is effected by the transfer of those credits, through the medium of foreign or domestic bills of exchange.

A small portion only is paid in currency; for when the balance of indebtedness is large, an extension of credit is generally granted. In large transactions, even not of a commercial nature, such as the purchase of land, it will be found that the payments are also principally made by the transfer of credits accumulated for that purpose, and rarely to a large amount in specie.

The deposits in banks are but occasionally made in specie. They generally consist of transfers of credit from banks, or arise from a note owned by the party, and discounted in his favor. Whatever their origin may be, they are credits opened in the books of banks, in favor of individuals to whom they are payable on demand. And as payments between country and country, or district and district, are effected by the transfer of credits through the medium of bills of exchange, so also payments in all the transactions of any importance, between inhabitants of the same city or district, are effected by checks on the banks, that is to say, by the transfer of those bank credits which are called deposits.

These checks, like bills of exchange, may be considered as a substitute for currency; or, as a special currency, between dealers and dealers, when the credit in bank (deposit) is in favor of a dealer; between consumers and dealers, when the deposit has been made by a person not in active business. They differ from bank issues, in that they are not received, as bank notes are, as a full payment of a debt; and that, if not paid by the bank, the drawer is still responsible. The bank note is taken in payment solely from the general confidence reposed in the bank; the check, from the special confidence placed in the drawer.

But the deposits, or cash credits on the books of a bank, are a liability of the bank payable on demand like bank notes. In reference to such bank, the actual issues and deposits, though not always pressing on it at the same time and to the same extent, are liabilities of the same nature, and for which provision must be equally made.

Of the great benefits derived from these deposits, considered as substitutes for currency, and effecting payments with much greater facility than can be done with the precious metals, there can be no doubt. The perpetual transfers of twelve millions of dollars of individual deposits, that is to say, of credits in favor of individuals, in the several banks of the city of New-York, together with one or two millions of notes of a large denomination, which pass daily from bank to bank, and make no part of the general circulation, are sufficient to effect annually payments amounting to about twelve hundred millions. It appears by the late statements of the Bank of France, that although the private deposits of that institution do not exceed seventy millions of francs, the transfers (*mouvemens*) of these were sufficient to effect, in six months, payments (*liquidations*) amounting to seventeen hundred and forty-two millions. By an analogous, though not perfectly similar, process, the actual daily payment of an ultimate balance of two or three hundred thousand pounds in specie or in notes of the Bank of England, effects daily payments of four or five millions sterling in the clearing-house of the London bankers. The same benefits were derived from the ancient

Bank of Amsterdam ; and the Bank of Hamburg is founded on the same principle. Neither of these institutions ever issued paper money, or was even a bank of discount. It was only as banks of deposit, and solely by the transfers of credits substituted for payments in specie, that they accomplished the purpose of discharging, with increased facility, almost all the engagements growing out of the commercial transactions of those two cities.

It is important to observe that, if all our State banks were converted into banks only of discount and deposit, but not of issue, the failure of one or more of them could affect only the depositors, and not the community at large ; and that, if even the supposition of a general failure by all such banks were admissible, it would only derange the beneficial system of transfers of credit, but would not affect the standard of value, which, since no paper currency had been put in circulation, would, for the community, continue to be the legal coin of the country, and nothing else ; whilst, under the existing system, the deposits, blended, as liabilities payable on demand, with the issues of the banks, contribute to endanger their safety, and may occasionally, in our great cities, cause a suspension of specie payments.

On the other hand, since those deposits would still exist and produce the same beneficial effects, if there were no other banks but only of discount and deposit, it does not appear correct to reckon their amount as part of the additional capital acquired by the establishment of our banks of issue. It may, however, be objected, that in rejecting, as not belonging to banks of issue, the advantages which might have been obtained by banks only of discount and deposit, it has been taken for granted that such private banks or joint stock banking companies, issuing no paper currency, might be established and sustained in America. This position may be denied ; and it may be asserted, that banks giving sufficient accommodation to the productive industry of the country could not exist here, unless they had the right to issue bank notes.

This assertion might have been quite correct fifty years ago, and is partly true even now. It must be admitted in the first place, that there are, as yet, but few men in the United States,

With a sufficient capital to carry on with safety banking operations, and fewer still who do not find more profitable employment for that capital. The necessity of concentrating for that
purpose small capitals, and of forming banking associations, is obvious: and although the shareholders in such companies are satisfied with dividends generally not exceeding the ordinary rate of
interest, and always falling short of the profits of a private
banker, the machinery of such institutions is much more expensive, and their gross profits must at least be sufficient to pay
the interest, to defray those expenses and to cover contingent
losses.

An examination of the statements of the State banks will
show, that the resources of those of the commercial cities, particularly of those with a large capital, consist principally of their
deposits; and that, though their profits would be somewhat diminished, they would be still sufficient to enable the banks to
continue their legitimate operations.

On the 1st of January, 1841, the twenty-two chartered banks
of the city of New York, with a capital of little more than
twenty millions of dollars, had more than twelve millions of
individual deposits, besides near two millions deposited by country or foreign banks, and a gross circulation of apparently about
five, but in fact of less than three millions (b). Their loans and
discounts exceeded twenty-seven millions, and the stocks owned
by them were less than three millions. Had they been only
banks of discount and deposit, the aggregate of their assets bearing interest, and amounting to thirty millions, would have been
lessened about three millions, or ten per cent. This would, in
the aggregate, have reduced their dividends from $6\frac{3}{4}$ to 6 per
cent. But those returns embraced several banks which have
incurred heavy losses, and made no dividend. The sound

(b) They had in their possession on the same day more than three millions, in·
notes of each other or of other banks. The returns of the city banks are made
before they have exchanged the notes of each other received during the day. On
the 19th February, 1834, the apparent circulation of nineteen city banks amounted
to 4,740,000, and the actual circulation after the exchanges, to 3,040,000. (Report
of Union Committee.)—The daily payments in notes and checks into the several
city banks amount to about 4,000,000, in ordinary times.

banks would still have divided at least seven per cent. which is amply sufficient; and, by converting the stocks owned by them into discounts, there would have been no diminution in the amount of their commercial loans.

On the other hand, the country banks, under which denomination must be included those of all the interior States and of the interior parts of the other States, depend principally on their circulation; and although, in many places, the dividends have been extravagant, yet it must be acknowledged that, if the bank notes were altogether suppressed, the banking capital now employed in the country would be considerably reduced, and become confined to those towns which are the principal centres of its commercial transactions.

Strong reasons might be adduced to show that such a reduction would ultimately be beneficial. It is extremely doubtful whether the banking system, with its indispensable strict punctuality, can, under any circumstances, be beneficially applied to purely agricultural purposes. The only material improvement which has during the last fifty years taken place in Virginia, her having become one of the first wheat-growing States, cannot be ascribed to her banks. In every other respect, what has she gained by the circulation of bank notes; and what progress has she made, since the introduction of banks, in agriculture, manufactures, commerce, or population? The situation of the planters who cultivate the fresh and fertile soil of Alabama and of Mississippi, affords an irrefragable proof of the calamities inflicted on an agricultural country by an exaggerated banking system, and by excessive issues.

The inquiry might be pursued farther. Yet as those evils may be ascribed to the abuse and not to the temperate use of banks and bank paper, and as the advantages of banking are now considered independent of the evils it produces, it may for the present be conceded that banks purely of discount and deposit could not, in the interior parts of the country, be generally substituted for banks of issue; and that, in computing the additional capital acquired by the banking system, the deposits in country banks may be added to the amount of issues. This would make the whole addition to the capital ninety instead of sixty millions. The estimate is founded on the present reduced amount of issues and deposits, and not on that of the years 1836–37, when they were, together, fifty per cent. greater (c).

The increase of capital, be it more or less, appears to be, if not absolutely the only, at least the principal advantage derived from a paper currency. It has been denied by some, that even this did confer any benefit on the community at large. It has been asserted that the whole profit was engrossed by the issuers, or, at best, shared only by those whom the issues of paper enabled to obtain additional loans of money; that this profit, instead of being in any way advantageous to the community, was made at its expense; that it made the rich richer, and the poor poorer; and that the whole system was one of fraud and iniquity.

It is not perceived on what ground the charge can be sustained, unless it be insisted that the state of society, in its present civilization, is so unjust and nefarious that every addition to the capital of a nation, every increase of national wealth, produces the same baneful effects, and is a positive evil. That such increase, when effected by the introduction of a paper currency, is always dangerous, and may be attended with most calamitous consequences, is fully admitted. But if a complete guarantee could be obtained that the paper currency would always remain equal in value to gold and silver, the danger would be avoided. And so long as this is the fact, the additional capital, thus supplied, operates in the same manner, and is attended with the same effects, as any other increase of national wealth.

The immediate benefits of any acquisition of wealth or capital

---

(c) In the report of the Secretary of the Treasury, of April, 1840, Statement JJ, page 1374, it is thus estimated:

	1st January, 1837.	1st January, 1840.
Actual Circulation	112,652,000	86,170,000
Deposits	127,397,000	75,696,000
	240,049,000	161,866,000

Our estimate is as follows:

Actual Circulation	86,000,000
Country Deposites	37,000,000
	123,000,000
Deduct Specie in Banks	33,000,000
Additional Capital gained by our Banking system	90,000,000

most certainly accrue to those who have acquired it. This acquisition makes the rich richer, or, to speak more correctly, particularly in this case, it increases the number of those who become rich or independent. But this is not done at the expense of the community: the process does not make the poor poorer. On the contrary, every increase of capital puts in activity a greater quantity, and, all other things remaining equal, has a tendency to enhance the wages of labor. This is consistent with theory, and confirmed by experience. Production is always increased in proportion to the increased wealth of a country, labor is better paid, commodities are rendered cheaper, and more comforts brought within the reach of the poor. In America, the quantity of uncultivated land, a dormant capital which perpetually calls for labor in order to render it productive, is the primary cause of that greatest of all the worldly blessings this nation enjoys. Manual labor is better remunerated in America than in any other country. But even here, circulating capital, that capital which consists of accumulated consumable commodities, is necessary before labor can be employed. The agricultural laborer, who, without any capital, migrates westwardly to a new settled country, is immediately employed, and receives competent wages. Yet the product of his labor does not become available till after the ensuing crop: he must in the meanwhile be fed and clothed; and this would be impossible, and he would have no means of existence, had not the farmer who employs him an accumulated capital sufficient for that purpose.

Since the principal advantage of a paper currency consists in the additional capital it supplies, such currency is most useful, above all most wanted, but unfortunately a more dangerous expedient, in those countries and places where there is the least amount of circulating capital as compared to the demand for it. This is eminently the case in newly settled countries, with a rapidly increasing population. We find accordingly the local governments of America perpetually resorting to emissions of paper money under the colonial regimen; and that, at this moment, the excess of issues occurs principally in the Western States, and generally wherever country banks have been established.

The converse of the proposition would seem to be equally

true, and that, in countries saturated with capital, the addition to it by the issue of bank notes does not compensate for the perpetual fluctuations and alarms growing out of that system. There may be substantial reasons, why Great Britain perseveres in it: they have not been fully explained, and are not understood by the writer of this essay. But wherever a paper currency has been introduced, the permanency of its value should be the indispensable condition of its existence.

The unanimous assent of all civilized nations has made gold and silver their universal circulating medium and standard of value. By forbidding any other legal tender in payment of debts, the constitution of the United States, without absolutely excluding every other circulating medium, has imperatively rendered the precious metals the only standard of value. The substitution of a paper for a gold or silver currency is therefore admissible, only on the express condition, that it shall always be equal in value to the legal coin of which it is the representative; and that equality cannot be maintained, unless the paper be at all times convertible, on demand, into such coin, at its nominal value. Any deviation from that principle is unjust in itself, and an evasion of the constitutional provision. It is a violation of existing contracts, renders all subsequent engagements uncertain, destroys confidence, and impairs private and public credit.

Banks of issue, deposits and discounts have therefore a double duty to perform; first, to be at all times ready to pay their notes and deposits in specie, so as to preserve the constitutional standard of value; secondly, to give accommodations by advances to the productive industry of the country; for which purpose, indeed, they were instituted. But the first duty is positive and absolute: they are bound in the first instance to fulfil their engagements: it is the express condition on which the banks were permitted to issue paper: they have no right whatever to issue a depreciated currency. The second duty is discretionary and subordinate to the first: it can be exercised rightfully, only so far as can be done without running the risk of placing themselves in a situation that would put it out of their power to fulfil their engagements.

These two duties are therefore to some extent contradictory;

and the question has been agitated in England, whether they ought not and might not be separated. This will not be now discussed, as it is believed that, at least for the present, such separation would, as a general measure, be impracticable in the United States.

The present situation of the banking system has proved, but too conclusively, the general inclination to increase immoderately the banking capital and the number of banks; and also the general tendency of all the banks to extend their loans and discounts beyond what prudence and their primary duty would dictate; and it is believed that this defect is inherent to all joint stock banking companies.

Not only is it the interest of the shareholders, so long as they are not personally responsible beyond the amount of their shares, to obtain as large a dividend as possible, but the evil grows out of the manner in which joint stock companies must be governed. The direction must necessarily be placed in the hands of a few men, who have comparatively but little interest in the bank. Most of them are selected amongst men in active business, in order that they may be able to judge of the solidity of the paper offered for discount; and as they are not paid, it is impossible to expect that they should attend without deriving some compensation for the sacrifice of a portion of their precious time. This may consist in part from the discounts they obtain for themselves, which may always be kept within reasonable bounds. But the power and consideration attached to the office can be obtained only by granting favors; whilst, on the contrary, a refusal renders the directors unpopular. To this may be added a want of sufficient moral responsibility. The honorable merchant, who would feel disgraced by his own individual failure, is not affected by that of the bank of which he may be a director. It is well known that this general observation does not apply to bank directors alone, but to all public bodies. Of all the causes, however, which contribute to an improper extent of discounts, the most general and efficient, the most prolific source of the errors of bank directors, is the natural sympathy which they feel for men who are engaged in similar pursuits to their own. It may, upon the whole, be affirmed, that banks, though money lenders, are in fact governed rather by the borrowers than by the lenders.

It is known to every body, that the liabilities payable on demand, of the best conducted banks, are always necessarily much greater than their immediately available resources. In order to be sustained, not only must they enjoy general confidence, but their existence depends on the will of the commercial community. If, in a time of extraordinary pressure, those who are deeply embarrassed should, under great excitement, either from selfish motives, or rather from error in judgment, think it desirable to shelter themselves under a general relaxation, they may, if sufficiently numerous and influential, force, and have in fact occasionally lent their aid in forcing, banks to suspend, or to persevere in suspending specie payments.

Such a general suspension is therefore the natural general disease of the banking system; it is that to be most guarded against, as it is also in its consequences the most fatal; much more so than the occasional failures of some individual banks, which, though an evil, are rare (*d*), local, and not contagious.

The example of the suspension by the Bank of England, which continued more than twenty years, has sometimes been adduced in proof that such an event was a very tolerable evil, and an expedient to which resort might occasionally be had.

What were the inducements of the British Government for resorting to that expedient in the year 1797, after having, during the next preceding one hundred years, carried on several wars without having found such measure necessary, and what actual advantages, political, financial, or commercial, she derived from it, it is not necessary or perhaps proper to discuss in this place. But it cannot be doubted that that act dissolved the charm; and that, since the resumption, the alarms and inconveniences connected with paper issues have been increased and aggravated by the feeling that, as the bank had once, so it might again suspend its specie payments. The effect in America has been, to familiarize the idea that a continued suspension might become

---

(*d*) This will be adverted to hereafter. Not one of the city banks of New York has failed since the year 1829.

the ordinary state of things, and that banks might fail without becoming bankrupts.

But the situation of the United States is very different from that of Great Britain, when a general suspension of the banks takes place. Great Britain is governed by one, and the United States by twenty-six independent legislatures. There a single bank controls the whole system ; here it is left at the mercy of an indefinite number of banks, independent of each other. Accordingly, the issues of the irredeemable notes of the Bank of England were at first kept within reasonable bounds, and the depreciation for several years was almost insensible. It increased gradually ; and during the years 1811–1815, the notes of the Bank had sunk from 20 to 25 per cent. below their nominal value. Even under more favorable circumstances, the evils which follow a departure from sound principles could not ultimately be averted.

The great difference, however, between the effects of a general suspension in the two countries respectively, is the uniformity of the depreciation in England, whilst the reverse is the case in America. The notes of the Bank of England were alone substituted there for the precious metals, as a legal tender. All the other banks of issue, the private bankers of England, and the joint stock companies of Scotland, were still obliged, when called upon, to redeem their own issues in notes of the Bank of England, or, which was the same thing, in drafts on London. Whatever the depreciation might be, whatever evils might be caused by its fluctuation, still that depreciation was at the same time the same throughout every district of Great Britain and of Ireland : it affected in a direct manner all foreign exchanges and transactions : it had no immediate and direct effect on domestic exchanges.

In the United States the depreciation is different at the same time in the different States, in different districts of the same State, and occasionally in the different banks of the same district. The effect is not confined to foreign exchanges ; the different and fluctuating depreciation affect domestic exchanges, and every species of domestic transactions. Those evils have increased with the protracted continuance of the suspension, and the effect on the moral feeling of the community has been most lamentable.

When banks suspend specie payments, their debtors have a right to discharge the debt in the depreciated paper of those institutions. But, because the banks offer to pay their own debts with the same paper, it is not perceived whence the right accrues to individuals to pursue the same course towards each other. They have not the legal right, since, in case of a suit, the debt can only be discharged in the legal coin of the country: nothing but gold or silver is by the constitution a legal tender. Morally, every debtor is still bound to pay his creditors, the suspended banks only excepted, in coin, or at least in the depreciated currency at its market price in gold or silver. It happens, however, that the great mass of merchants, who reside in the same place, being at the same time debtors and creditors, find it more convenient still to pay each other by the transfer of bank deposits, or to take and pay the bank paper at its nominal value. This, whilst confined to those who have a common interest in pursuing that course, may not be improper, and is convenient. But it is utterly unjust towards those who are creditors at home and debtors abroad, towards all those who have only debts to collect and none to pay, or who, if they have payments to make as consumers, are obliged to purchase at enhanced prices. The loss falls, heavily and most unjustly, on those who live on wages, which do not advance with the enhanced prices of articles of consumption, but which, on the contrary, generally fall during a period of universal derangement.

The injustice is still greater between those different cities and States where the depreciation is not the same. When the parties have failed or are unable at once to meet their engagements, amicable arrangements must take place; and the creditors, in such cases, are satisfied to receive what the debtor can pay. But those debtors, residing in States or places where the local currency is most depreciated, who can pay, now begin to think that, because they pay and are paid at home with that currency, they are absolved from the obligation to pay in any other way their creditors who reside in other places or States. It amounts to this; you must receive this depreciated paper at par, or you may institute a suit, and the creditor, who knows the expenses and delays of the law, and who must realize his active debts in order to meet his own engagements, is compelled to submit. In process of time, the people generally acquiesce ; the banks seem to forget altogether in what consists their primary duty, and, under pretence of alleviating the distress, consult only their own convenience. The same feeling at last penetrates into the legislative halls ; and the State legislatures, which at first had appeared disposed to enforce a prompt return of the banks to their duty, yield and authorize, sometimes even encourage, an almost indefinite continuance of the suspension.

It would be painful to pursue the subject any farther, and to advert to the recklessness, gross neglect, inconceivable mismanagement, amounting to a breach of trust, to the disgraceful and heretofore unheard-of frauds, which have occasionally occurred, or to that which is perhaps still worse, the apathy or lenity with which those enormities are viewed.

It may with truth be affirmed, that the present situation of the currency of the United States is worse than that of any other country. The value even of the irredeemable paper money of Russia has, during the last forty years, been more uniform ; and in its fluctuations, the tendency has been to improve and not to deteriorate that value. No hesitation is felt in saying that, whatever may be the presumed advantages of a moderate use of a paper currency, convertible into specie on demand, to have no issue of paper would be far preferable to the present state of things. The object of this essay is to inquire whether any practicable remedies can be applied to the system.

CAUSES AND INCIDENTS OF THE BANK SUSPENSIONS.

ALL active, enterprising, commercial countries are necessarily subject to commercial crises. A series of prosperous years almost necessarily produces overtrading. Those revolutions will be more frequent and greater in proportion to the spirit of enterprise, and to the extension or abuse of credit. But, however prices may be affected, and whatever may be the evils growing out of the crisis, there will be no violation of contracts, and the standard of value will not be affected in countries where there is no paper currency. The danger of a suspension of specie payments, which immediately deranges that standard, is necessarily increased in proportion to the amount of issues of paper of that description ; and that amount depends, in a great degree, on the denomination of the bank notes permitted to be issued as currency, on the number of the banks of issue. and, in the United States, on the capital invested in bank stock (e).

All these dangerous elements are found united in a greater degree in the United States than in any other commercial country. The large field opened for enterprise, the free institutions of the country, and the indomitable energy of the people, have produced results astonishing and without parallel in the history of other nations. A wilderness has within forty years been converted into the abode of six millions of civilized and most industrious people. Expensive communications have been opened, superior in extent and importance to those of continental Europe. The American commerce and navigation extend to every quarter of the globe, and are inferior to those of no other country but England. But there are evils which, to a certain extent, appear to be the necessary consequence of a state of high commercial prosperity, and which in America are much

---

(e) The capital of the banks is, in the United States, universally loaned to traders : generally speaking, the European banks and bankers lend only the amount of their circulation and deposits. The capitals of the Bank of England and of the Bank of France are vested in public securities.

increased by the want of a capital proportionate to the extent of commercial and other undertakings.

Overtrading has been the primary cause of the present crisis in America. Abundant proofs of the fact are found in the immoderate use of foreign credit, as well as in the excessive importations and sales of public lands in the years 1834–37.

Of imports—

During the nine years, 1822–1830, the average annual amount was $59,000,000

" three " 1831–1833, " " " 83,000,000

" four " 1834–1837, " " " 130,000,000

In " 1836 alone, " " " 168,000,000

The average annual excess of imports over the exports amounted to four millions during the first nine years; to eighteen millions during the three next ensuing; to thirty-four millions during the four last, and to sixty-one millions in the year 1836 alone.

The average annual sales of public lands, which, during the first nine years, did not exceed 1,300,000 dollars, and which during the years 1831–35, had reached 4,500,000, amounted in 1835 to seventeen, and in 1836 to twenty-five millions. Speculations in unimproved town lots, mines, and every description of rash undertakings, increased at the same rate.

The fault, or error, originated with the people themselves. The traders and speculators have attempted to ascribe their disasters altogether to legislative acts; to those of the Administration or to other collateral causes, which have indeed aggravated the evils, but the effects of some of which have been exaggerated. Still, although it would be improper to abridge the freedom of action which all individuals should be permitted to enjoy, it is certain that the spirit of enterprise did not require any artificial stimulus.

The prodigious increase of State banks was the result of State legislation. From the 1st of January 1830 to the 1st of January 1837, three hundred new banks were created, with a capital of one hundred and forty-five millions of dollars. This increase was undoubtedly due to the eagerness for capital applicable to commercial accommodations or other purposes. It may be ascribed in part to the expiration of the charter of the Bank of the United States, and to the anticipation of that event. It was thought necessary, in some places, to fill the chasm in capital and commercial accommodations that must follow the dissolution of that institution. The same effect had been produced in the years 1810–16, on the occurrence of the expiration of the charter of the former national bank; and in both cases the increase far exceeded the apprehended loss and the wants of the country.

The great increase of banks took place accordingly in the Western States, where capital was most wanted. During the years above mentioned, the increase in the banking capital of the North-Western States amounted to near twenty, and that of the South-Western to almost fifty-five millions of dollars (*f*).

But that increase was far beyond what might have been wanted for useful purposes. Near three-fifths of the foreign merchandize imported into the United States are imported into New York. That city is also the principal place of deposit for the sale of the domestic manufactures of the country; and it is also the centre of all the monied transactions of the United States. In the year 1837, the capital of all the banks of that city hardly exceeded twenty millions of dollars; and it was sufficient for all the legitimate operations of commerce. When an unexpected increase of the public deposits enabled and induced those banks to expand their discounts beyond their ordinary rate, that excess excited over-trading, and was applied to extraordinary and dangerous speculations.

In order to obtain or to assist in obtaining the capital wanted for the new banks, for internal improvements, and for some other miscellaneous purposes, debts were incurred by several States, amounting from 1830 to 1838 to near one hundred and fifty millions of dollars. The debt contracted by the Atlantic States was almost entirely for internal improvements; no part of it for banking purposes, and it fell little short of sixty millions. That contracted by the North-Western States amounted to about thirty-eight millions, of which thirty-one millions five hundred

---

(*f*) The designations of the Secretary of the Treasury of the United States are adopted here, as convenient for reference. According to these, Ohio, Indiana, Illinois, Michigan, Missouri, and Kentucky, are the North-Western; and Tennessee, Alabama, Mississippi, Louisiana, and Arkansas, the South-Western States.

thousand dollars were for internal improvements, and the residue for banking capital. That incurred by the South-Western States was about fifty-two millions, of which more than forty-four millions were for banking capital, and the residue for internal improvements.

The population of the United States, by the census of 1840, exceeds seventeen millions, of whom ten millions seven hundred and sixty thousand are in the Atlantic, four millions one hundred and thirty thousand in the North-Western, and two millions two hundred and thirty thousand in the South-Western States.

It may be observed, that the reason why so much more capital was applied in the South-Western than in the North-Western States to banking purposes, is to be found in the difference of capital wanted for the employment of slave and free labor respectively. The northern farmer advances no more than twelve months wages to the laborer he employs. The southern planter, who wishes to increase the product of his land, must advance the price of the slave himself, which amounts perhaps to five or six times the net product of his annual labor. The application of banking accommodation to purely agricultural purposes has accordingly been much greater, and has been attended with far more fatal effects, in the South-Western States, than in any other section of the Union. But even the State debts, created for internal improvements, have co-operated in aggravating the evils under which we now labor. Not only were their proceeds applied to purposes of which the returns were slow and uncertain, but they also supplied the means of paying balances or obtaining credits abroad. Thus, extravagant importations were encouraged, whilst, at the same time, some of those stocks became objects of speculation at home, in which individuals and banks were involved, and which proved injurious to all the parties concerned; to the States, as well as to the purchasers. Several of the States neglected to provide a revenue sufficient to pay the annual interest accruing on their debts. Additional loans were resorted to for that purpose ; and occasionally forced loans were required by the States from the banks, which lessened their resources, and had a tendency to produce or to protract the suspension of specie payments.

It has ever been the opinion of the writer of this essay, that a public debt was always an evil, to be avoided whenever practicable; hardly ever justifiable except in time of war; to be resorted to even then with sobriety, and never to be incurred without providing at the same time an additional revenue, sufficient to pay the interest and ultimately to discharge the principal of the debt. A long life of experience and observation has produced an intimate conviction of the soundness of those principles. Independently of the great, manifest and permanent evils inflicted by the abuse of public credit, every public debt absorbs a capital which otherwise would have been applied to purposes as least as productive as those for which the debt was incurred. It has a tendency, perhaps, more than any other cause, to concentrate the national wealth in the hands of a small number of individuals. The interest must at all times be paid by taxes extracted from the proceeds of the productive labor of the community; and it feeds the drones of society.

These considerations do not by any means justify the suggestion, that a nation is not bound to discharge the engagements contracted, even perhaps improvidently, by its Government. A son who inherited a large estate might, with as much propriety, think himself under no obligation to discharge the liens on his inheritance. In the United States, where such engagements have always been contracted by the immediate representatives of the people, and those representatives elected by universal suffrage, there is not even the color of a pretence for the supposition, that the people are not bound by the acts of those representatives. Any such suggestion should at once be indignantly dismissed as dishonest and disgraceful. The errors of legislation may be regretted; but they bind the nation.

The early agitation of the question respecting the renewal of the charter of the Bank of the United States, the veto of the bill passed by the two Houses of Congress for that purpose, and the removal of the public deposits long before the expiration of the charter, are the principal acts of the executive branch of the General Government which may have affected the state of the currency.

Previous to any of these, there had been an improper interference, on the part of the Treasury Department, in the choice of some of those officers whose appointment did by the charter belong exclusively to the directors of the mother bank. This, instead of strengthening, had a tendency to weaken the natural and legitimate influence of that department over the general management of the bank: it was an unfortunate and novel introduction of party feelings into the fiscal concerns of the nation.

The President had an undoubted right to put his veto on a law which renewed the charter of an institution which, in his opinion, was not constitutional. But there was no necessity for the early attack on an institution, the charter of which did not expire till two years after the end of the term for which the President had been elected.

The currency of the country was as sound in the year 1829, as may probably be expected under any system which admits the substitution of paper for the precious metals. It seems to have been unwise to interfere with this, without having previously weighed the probable consequences and without having prepared a proper substitute. The President indeed suggested the possibility, not of dispensing altogether with a national bank, but of establishing one founded on different principles. It appears, however, that he entertained only general views on the subject, and had not adopted any determinate plan of action. In point of fact, no such plan or substitute was ever offered; and the final result was to leave the currency at the mercy of State banks and State legislation.

The immediate consequences were, to encourage the creation of new State banks, to place the Government and the Bank of the United States in an unnatural hostile attitude to each other, to change the character of that institution, which could not previously be justly charged with any wilful misconduct, and to convert every discussion connected with the subject into pure party questions.

The early removal of the public deposits seems to have been unnecessary; and the reasons alleged for it were altogether insufficient. On a similar previous occasion, those deposites had been removed only a week prior to the expiration of the charter of the former Bank of the United States. Not the slightest inconvenience was felt on that account. And it may be generally observed, that the course pursued at that time by all parties, was such that the bank expired quietly without agitating the public mind. The subject did not, as of late, absorb every other public consideration, and become the great political or party question of the country.

The specie circular, issued at a subsequent date, and which directed the payments to the Treasury for public lands, and only for public lands, to be made in specie, appears to the writer of this essay to have been improper. The order was issued several months before the suspension of specie payments by the banks. Whether the President thought the practice of paying in notes of specie-paying banks, generally acquiesced in for a period of more than forty years, to be consistent with or contrary to the constitution, the rule should have been general. It is not seen on what principle two different rules were established, and a distinction made between payments into the Treasury, on account of duties on importations, and those for purchases of public lands; between those who claimed lands, by entries according to law, or by actual settlement.

The only effect of that measure, so far as it has been ascertained, was to cause a drain of specie on the banks of New York, at a time when it was important that that point should have been strengthened. It transferred specie from the place where it was most wanted in order to sustain the general currency of the country, to places where it was not wanted at all. It thus accumulated so much in Michigan, that, whilst it was travelling from New York to Detroit, the Secretary of the Treasury was obliged to draw heavily on Michigan, in favor of New York and other sea-ports. Had no interference taken place, and had the transactions of individuals been left to their natural course, it is clear that the lands would have been paid for in Eastern funds, and that the double transmission of specie, where it took place, would at least have been avoided.

Independently of the objections to which premature and intermediate measures may be liable, the charges against the President, for having interfered in the currency, resolve themselves into the single fact of having prevented the renewal of the charter of the Bank of the United States. The direct and immediate effects cannot be correctly ascertained; but they have been greatly exaggerated by party spirit. That he found the currency of the country in a sound, and left it in a deplorable state, is true: but he cannot certainly be made responsible for the aberrations and misdeeds of the Bank under either of its charters. The unforeseen, unexampled, accumulation of the public revenue was one of the principal proximate causes of the disasters that ensued. It cannot be ascribed either to the President or to any branch of Government ; and its effects *might* have been the same, whether the public deposits were in the State banks, or had been left in the national bank, organized and governed as that was.

By the provisions of the act, respecting the tariff, generally called the Compromise Act, the reduction of the duties, to the amount deemed sufficient, after the final payment of the public debt, to meet the national expenditures, was made gradual and could at first operate but slowly. But in order to prevent the accumulation of monies in the Treasury, every foreign article which did not compete with domestic industry was made duty free ; and this measure seems to have been deemed sufficient by all parties to effect the purpose. This proved to have been a mistake. It may be that the repeal of the duties on certain articles encouraged too large importations in that respect ; but all the causes which excited overtrading were in full operation. And it is probable that the danger of an accumulated revenue did not sufficiently attract the attention of the legislature.

A revenue, consisting exclusively of duties on importations and of the proceeds of the sales of public lands, must necessarily be subject to great fluctuations ; and such had been experienced in the year 1817, and at other times. But they were not felt, and therefore not particularly attended to, so long as, in addition to an annual fixed appropriation, all the surplus revenues were appropriated and applied to the payment of the principal of the public debt. That payment was the safety-valve which prevented any dangerous accumulation of monies in the Treasury. Whether any systematic arrangement, connected with such of the expenditures for the defence of the country, as may be lessened or increased according to circumstances, might not have been devised, is an important question which will hereafter well deserve the consideration of Government. No such prospective measures, however, had been deemed necessary ; and more than forty millions of accumulated revenue became deposited in the State banks, thus affording a new extraordinary fund for bank accommodations and expansions. These were unfortunately encouraged by the Treasury Department, which seems, on this occasion, to have yielded to the general clamor of those who represented the withdrawal of the capital and loans of the Bank of the United States as threatening ruin to commerce. Apprehensive that the deposite banks of the city of New York could not, on account of the limitations in their charters, sufficiently extend their discounts, the Secretary of the Treasury had, before the Act of June 1836, directed those institutions to lend a part of the public deposits to the other city banks.

This course was sanctioned by that act, which directed that the public deposits in any bank should not exceed three-fourths of its capital; and the law, by directing that the banks should pay interest whenever those deposits exceeded a certain sum, rendered their partial application to discounts actually necessary.

But Congress, justly alarmed at that great increase of the public moneys in the Treasury, thought proper to distribute it among the several States. The propriety of this measure, and its consistency with the spirit of the constitution, may be questioned. Subsequent events have shown that the amount intended to be withdrawn from the Treasury was too large, and that, as might have been anticipated, the revenue of the next ensuing years fell short of the current expenditures. But, viewed in reference only to the banking system and to the paper currency of the country, the process, though protracted and spread over fifteen months, was much too prompt. The Legislature was not, and could not indeed be aware, how slow and gradual the diminution of discounts must be, in order that universal distress may not ensue.

The public deposits in the city banks of New York amounted to fourteen millions of dollars. At the same time that they were ordered to be withdrawn, the state of the money market in England arrested the progressive and exaggerated credits heretofore granted to the American merchants, and on the continuance of which they had relied. The consequent necessity of making large remittances to England, whilst those expected from the South-West began to fail, and the simultaneous withdrawal of the public deposits, may be considered as the principal proximate causes of the suspension of specie payments in 1837. In the city of New York the great destruction of capital by the fire of December 1835, frauds committed on one of the principal banks, and some other local incidents, co-operated in producing that result. The Bank of the United States had but little share in it.

It would be idle to inquire whether, if the charter of that institution had been renewed, and if it had been the sole place of deposit of the forty millions of public moneys, the suspension might have been prevented. That would have depended entirely on the manner in which the bank might have been administered.

That institution had ceased to be a regulator of the currency as early as the years 1832–33, when its discounts and other investments were increased from fifty-five to sixty-five millions, that is to say, at the rate of 85 per cent. beyond its capital; whilst those of the sound banks of our great commercial cities did not exceed the rate of 60 per cent. beyond their capital. It is not necessary to inquire whether this expansion was the natural consequence of the course of trade, whether the Bank of the United States was in any degree influenced by considerations connected with its own existence, or whether the machinery carried away the directors instead of being governed by them. It is obvious, that it is only by keeping its discounts at a lower rate than those of the State banks, that these can be its debtors; and that it is only by enforcing the payment of the balances, that it can keep them within bounds, and thus regulate the currency. A contrary course will induce the State banks to enlarge their own discounts, and will engender excessive issues, followed by necessary contractions and unavoidable distress.

But a great change had taken place in the situation of that bank. On its dissolution in March 1836, it accepted a new charter on onerous conditions from the State of Pennsylvania, and, contrary to what had been anticipated, the greater part of its circulation was almost immediately returned to it for redemption. It now appears, by a statement of its affairs dated 1st Feb. 1836, and laid at the time before the stockholders, that its actual circulation amounted on that day to $24,360,000, and its deposits to $4,400,000. On the 1st Jan. 1837, the actual circulation was reduced to $11,450,000, and the deposits to $2,330,000. Those funds on which, in addition to its capital, the bank must rely for making or continuing its discounts, were in ten months reduced from near twenty-nine to about fourteen millions, or more than one half. It was impossible to have, within that short period, reduced the discounts to the same extent. Accordingly the bank had already incurred other liabilities not payable on demand, amounting to near seven millions of dollars; its specie had been lessened from $7,650,000 to $2,640,000; and it was as powerless and as unable to prevent the suspension as the other State banks. Its situation was not known to the banks of New York, when application for relief was, at the moment of the crisis, made by that city to that institution. The manner, however, in which the relief was granted did not weaken it.

It must be acknowledged that, great as was the distress during that winter, and notwithstanding all the ominous circumstances of the times, the danger of a general suspension was not anticipated by the banks or the merchants of New York, nor indeed, it seems, any where else, before the month of March 1837. From that time, the city banks made the most strenuous efforts to avert the event, and so successfully as to arrest the drain of specie, the amount of which in their vaults was not lessened between the first and the last day of April. The Comptroller of the State and the other Commissioners of the Canal Fund, on being applied to and made acquainted with the imminent impending danger, had also agreed to lend to the banks three millions five hundred thousand dollars of State Stocks, which they were authorised to issue, but the proceeds of which were wanted only gradually within the two or three ensuing years. The loan was on the express condition, that the Stocks of the State, which were then above par in England, should be used as remittances, and to that extent lessen the intense demand for specie for the same purpose. The necessity of a law, authorising the banks to purchase the Stock, caused an unavoidable delay, which prevented the execution of the agreement: for, on the very day on which the law was passed, the drain on the banks, which had gradually increased, became so intense, that they concluded the same night to suspend their specie payments. It cannot be affirmed that this drain was any thing more than the result of a general panic. Yet there were symptoms of combination in the manner in which it was conducted. Such were the situation and feelings of the banks throughout the whole country, that they all, without any exception, and almost without deliberation, instantaneously suspended, as fast as the mail could convey the intelligence of the suspension in New York.

The Legislature of New York was on the eve of adjourning when the suspension took place. Under the excitement of the moment, and without sufficient deliberation, a law was passed, commonly called the Suspension Act, altogether unnecessary, and in some respects mischievous.

By the general laws of the State, or by the charters of the several banks, it was already enacted, 1st, that whenever a bank suspended specie payment during ten days (*g*), it should thenceforth cease its operations, save only the collection and payment of its debts, unless, on application to the Chancellor or Circuit Judge, and an examination of its affairs, it was permitted by that officer to continue its operations; 2dly, that if, at the expiration of one year, the bank did not resume its payments, it should be deemed to have surrendered its rights, and be adjudged to be dissolved.

The Suspension Act released, for the term of one year, the banks from any forfeiture of their charters incurred on account of a suspension of specie payment. It left the general law to operate at the expiration of the year as before provided. Its only effect, in that respect, was to release the banks from the obligation of submitting the statement of their affairs to the Chancellor, and to allow them to continue their operations without his permission; reserving, however, the power already vested in the Bank Commissioners, to apply for an injunction in any special case, when the situation of the bank appeared to require it. This alteration was quite unnecessary. It would have been far more eligible to allow the general law to operate; and this special provision conferred no real benefit on the banks (*h*).

(*g*) The term for the old banks, whose charters were renewed about the year 1831, was three months.

(*h*) One bank alone, wishing to rest on the general, without any aid from a special law, applied to the Vice-Chancellor, and continued its operations by virtue of

The only other enactment of the law, intended to favor the banks, was that which placed them on the same footing as individuals, by allowing no costs in suits under fifty dollars. But nothing was more easy than to institute suits on ten five-dollar notes together, and the result was the same as if the enactment had not taken place. The city banks were compelled silently to withdraw their five-dollar notes from circulation: and the only effect was a substitution in the city circulation of notes worse than theirs.

In another respect the special law was injurious to the city banks, by compelling them to take in payment of their debts, the notes of the country banks.

But the moral effect of the law was bad. Though it had in reality made no alteration in the existing law, it had the appearance and was generally considered as sanctioning the suspension : and the act was quoted in other States, and used as a pretence for passing suspension laws of a very different character.

As soon, however, as the first shock was over, the banks of the city of New York adopted a course of action preparatory to an early resumption: and in the month of August, they addressed a circular letter to the principal banks of the other States, requesting their co-operation, and proposing a convention of delegates from the banks of the several States, for the purpose of agreeing on a uniform course of measures and on the time when the resumption should take place. The South-Western States were not ready for any immediate action. Encouraging answers were received from the other Western and from the Southern banks, as well as from some other quarters. The Boston banks would not commit themselves, but at the last moment appointed delegates. The banks of Philadelphia adopted a resolution, that it was inexpedient at that time to appoint delegates ; and the banks of Baltimore followed the same example.

---

his order to that effect. But the proof, that the banks did not want the act, is found in the fact that the Manhattan Company, which did not comply with any of its provisions, continued its operations, and passed through the ordeal with the same facility as the other banks.

The principal reason alleged by the Philadelphia banks for their refusal was ominous. They declared their belief that the general resumption of specie payments depended mainly, if not exclusively, on the action of Congress, without whose co-operation all attempts at a general system of payments in coin throughout this extensive country must be partial and temporary.

What was the action and co-operation of Congress which was then alluded to? The only subject of complaint at that time against Congress, in reference to the currency, was its refusal to renew the charter of the Bank of the United States. No other action on its part had been asked than a renewal of that charter, or the creation of a new bank. The employment of the old bank under its new charter, as the fiscal agent of Government, was perhaps contemplated. Whatever the object might be, any attempt, or appearance of an attempt, to coerce Congress by a wilful continuance of the suspension, was highly improper. The banks of New York insisted that, whatever might be the action of Congress on the currency, the duty of resuming remained the same, and must be performed by the banks. The Philadelphia banks ultimately appointed delegates to the convention, which met at New York on the 27th November 1837.

At that meeting, though allusion was still made to some expected action of Congress, it was principally urged, not that the banks were unprepared for resuming, but that the state of the country generally rendered a resumption inexpedient for the present, that the time had not yet come when a day for that purpose could be designated; and that the continuance of a hasty resumption would be precarious.

The banks of New York insisted, that it was monstrous to suppose that, if the banks were able to resume and to sustain specie payments, they should have any discretionary right to discuss the question, whether a more or less protracted suspension was consistent with their views of the condition and circumstances of the country. Numerous facts were adduced to prove the ability of the banks to resume, that the British debt was settled or postponed, that the danger of an extraordinary exportation of specie was now out of question, and that no other known causes existed, which could prevent a general, though not universal, resumption of specie payments within a very short period.

In allusion to the action of Congress, and in reply to the complaint, that the banks of New York had improperly persisted in calling the convention contrary to the opinion of those of Philadelphia, it was answered with frankness, that the objections of the Philadelphia banks, or, to speak more correctly, of the United States Bank of Pennsylvania, were viewed as nothing more nor less than as an intended protracted suspension for an indefinite period of time. In corroboration, the extraordinary conduct of that bank was alleged, in having put in circulation, since the suspension, a large amount of the notes of the late Bank of the United States, thus substituting the paper currency of a dead and irresponsible body for its own.

Although the convention was nearly divided, nothing more could be obtained than general professions, and a resolution to meet again in April, for the purpose of considering, and, if practicable, determining upon the day when specie payments might be resumed.

The conflict was clearly between the United States Bank of Pennsylvania and those of New York. The other banks of Philadelphia, though divided in opinion and sound, had yielded, and Baltimore had thought proper to follow the same course. On the other hand, the disposition of the North-Western and Southern States was generally favorable to an early resumption, though they seem to have apprehended that they might not be able to sustain specie payments, if Philadelphia and Baltimore persisted in suspending. No such apprehension was felt in the Eastern States. Yet the banks of Boston, though earnestly desirous that the resumption might be effected without delay, and ready to co-operate, did, in the two conventions, and to the last moment, sustain by their votes and influence the views of the United States Bank. Such were the baneful effects of party applied to the fiscal concerns of the nation, and such the consequence of that institution having become, or been generally viewed as, the great antagonist of the Administration and the rallying point of its opponents.

The banks of New York, determined in their course, had

persevered in measures which would have enabled them to resume nearly two months earlier than they did. The exchanges
had become decidedly favorable : and the agreement with the
Comptroller for a loan of the residue of the State Stocks, which
was renewed and concluded in November 1837, enabled them,
according to the express terms of the contract, to replenish
without difficulty their vaults with specie. Aware, however, of
the importance of a co-operation on the part of the other banks,
they had, in the first convention, in vain asked that an earlier
day should be appointed for the adjourned meeting, and then
waited for its result. It was soon ascertained, when that assembly met, that a simultaneous resumption could not be obtained :
and it was then only requested, that the convention should recommend an early day for that purpose. Fair as was the pro-
spect at first, the vote to recommend so late a day as the 1st of
January 1839, was carried ; and the banks of New York were
left to resume alone and without any assurance of an earlier co-
operation.

But the circumstances of the times were eminently propitious.
Not only had the foreign debt been settled or postponed, and all
the exchanges, whether domestic or foreign, become decidedly
favorable, but one million sterling in specie had been imported,
under the auspices of the Bank of England, through the agency
of a commercial house. The city banks resumed with more
than seven millions of dollars in specie ; their gross circulation
reduced to three millions, and their other liabilities payable on
demand considerably diminished. The public deposits of the
United States, which on the 1st of January 1837 exceeded ten
millions of dollars, had all been paid. Their loans and discounts,
amounting on the 1st of January 1837 to forty-six millions, had
been reduced to thirty-two. They had been admirably seconded
by the country banks of the State, whose specie and city funds
had been increased, and the circulation and discounts reduced
in the same proportion. Much credit is due to the Bank Commissioners for their efforts in promoting that result.

Above all, the sound and most powerful portion of the commerce of New York had now taken an active part in promoting
an immediate resumption. The Debtor Interest, which, combined with that of the United States Bank of Pennsylvania, and

with the mistaken views of some and the unfounded apprehensions of others, had constantly attempted to impede the course pursued by the banks, was silenced. They resumed, sustained by that general support of the commercial community and by that general confidence which are indispensable for the maintenance of specie payments. They resumed in good faith and in full, redeeming the country paper which, during the suspension, had become the general currency of the city; freely substituting their own circulation, and paying without distinction, when required, all their liabilities. The resumption was effected without the slightest difficulty; and it is but just to add, that no attempt was made to impede it, either by the United States Bank of Pennsylvania, or from any other quarter.

The banks of Boston, and generally of New England, were the first to adopt the same course. Public opinion, operating first on the Governor of Pennsylvania, compelled the United States Bank to resume in the month of July; and the example was soon followed South and West throughout almost all the States. That happy state of things was of short duration. In October 1839, the United States Bank again suspended its payments; and again the South and the West adopted, or were obliged to pursue, the same course. After a short and vain attempt on the part of that institution to resume in January last, we are again reduced to the same situation. Boston and the Eastern States, New York and the adjacent part of New Jersey, and of late Charleston, sustain specie payments. Every where else, with perhaps some insulated exceptions, there is no other currency but irredeemable paper, more or less depreciated; and the suspension is almost everywhere sanctioned by the State legislation.

The facility with which specie payments had been resumed had produced, in some quarters, the erroneous belief, that the country had entirely recovered from the injuries inflicted by years of overtrading and inflated prices. Commercial business was revived too early, and bank facilities were too easily granted. The foreign importations of the year 1839 again amounted to one hundred and sixty-two millions, the exports to one hundred and twenty-one, and the excess to forty millions. But the suspension of October 1839, and its consequences to this day, must be ascribed almost exclusively to the United States Bank.

It has already been seen that, before the 1st of January 1837, and within the first ten months of its new position as a State bank, its legitimate means of discounting, other than its capital, that is to say, its circulation and deposits, had been reduced from twenty-nine to fourteen millions. Deducting the necessary amount of specie, its available means applicable to discounts or other investments, did not, including its capital, exceed forty-seven millions. Indeed, the onerous conditions imposed by the State charter and the purchase, at an advance of fifteen per cent., of the seven millions held by the United States in the stock of the old bank, made the truly available means considerably less. In that situation, its loans and profits, under a wise and cautious administration, should have been reduced to the amount corresponding with the actual means.

Instead of pursuing that course, a bold attempt was made, as soon as the suspension of May 1837 had taken place, to take advantage of that state of things for commencing a system of operation, foreign to the ordinary and legitimate transactions of any bank, and which might eventually, according to the sanguine expectations of the projectors, control the whole commerce of the country, reinstate the circulation of the Bank, and restore its pristine preponderance. It is obvious that this could not be carried into effect, even if the result had been as propitious as it has proved to be fatal, without prolonging the general suspension of specie payments. It became the interest of the Bank that this should be the case; and here may probably be found the principal cause, not at the time suspected, of the course pursued in that respect by that institution.

As early as the month of June 1837, a considerable portion of the available funds of the Bank was diverted from their legitimate object, and, instead of being applied to the gradual reduction of its liabilities, was loaned to the president and other officers or directors of the Bank, in order to be employed in advances on cotton shipped to Europe. A special agency, in reference to that object, was established in London in the ensuing month of November. The advances were greatly increased, and continued during a period of near two years. Although no loss may have been incurred by the Bank, the gross impropriety of loans to such an amount to officers of the Bank, is not the less evident. The sequel is well known. Other improvident loans were made. The Bank over-loaded itself, by purchase, or otherwise, with stocks of every possible description. It has been alleged that it was not the fault of the administrators of the Bank, if those stocks subsequently fell in value. The fault consisted in having converted the Bank into a stock-jobbing association. In the meanwhile, as other means were wanted, an enormous debt was contracted abroad.

On the 1st of April 1839, the foreign debt of the Bank amounted to twelve millions eight hundred thousand dollars, and the various stocks owned by it to near twenty-three millions (*i*). Its credit had indeed been artificially sustained; and its stock was selling at a considerable advance. It was nevertheless on the verge of destruction. In August of the same year, it was compelled to issue post notes, which soon fell to a discount of more than one per cent. a month. In September, the Bank drew largely on Europe without funds, and partly without advice. In order, if possible, to provide funds for that object, and also, as has been acknowledged, for the purpose of breaking the banks of New York, payment of the bills thus sold in that city was suddenly required in specie, and the amount shipped to Europe. The attempt was a failure in both respects; the banks stood, and the bills were dishonored. On the 9th of October, the United States Bank suspended its payments; and it is not improper to observe that, a fortnight later, another attempt was made, under its auspices, by the debtor interest of New York, to compel the banks to expand their discounts and thus prepare the way for another general suspension. The banks, as might well be expected, unanimously refused to yield.

From that time, the fate of that institution was considered as sealed by every impartial observer. Nevertheless, the other banks of Philadelphia still persevered in sustaining it, and suffered it to become largely indebted to them. The State protracted its existence, and, as an equivalent, exacted new

(*i*) $6,300,000 of which, consisting principally of Mississippi and Michigan stocks, and previously contracted for, were not yet entered on the ledger.

loans from it. In the meanwhile, it could no otherwise meet its liabilities abroad than by new loans, obtained on onerous conditions; and in order to sustain its expiring credit, a resumption was at last deemed absolutely necessary.

For that purpose, the other banks of Philadelphia agreed to return five millions of its circulation held by them, and to take in lieu thereof, post notes, payable in about twelve months after date. They thought that a loan of two millions and a half would be sufficient to enable them to grant that accommodation, and that with such aid they would be able to resume and maintain specie payments. The loan was obtained principally in Boston, partly in New York. As it was principally paid in checks upon Philadelphia and in Baltimore funds, it added but little to the available resources.

Besides this postponement of five millions of its debt, the United States Bank was, rather unexpectedly, assisted by a further loan obtained abroad, which added more than three millions of dollars to its immediately available resources. The attempt to resume nevertheless failed; and it was impossible that it should not have failed. The element indispensable for sustaining any bank, *confidence*, was utterly lost. It seems incredible that it should not have been foreseen, that, as soon as the United States Bank paid in specie, every person who held its notes would instantaneously seize the opportunity of converting them into cash (k).

The principal liabilities of the United States Bank, payable on demand, consisted of more than thirteen millions and a half of bank notes and post notes, which, by the arrangement with the other Philadelphia banks, were

Reduced to about..	7,650,000
Due to banks of the several States..	3,250,000
Due to individual depositors...	2,970,000
Guarantee of bonds of Planters Bank, &c.....................................	240,000
	$14,110,000

(k) The opinion of the writer of this essay was asked, at the time when application was made in behalf of the Philadelphia banks for the loan mentioned in the text. It was decidedly against a compliance with the request; and the reason assigned, was the total impossibility, on the part of the United States

During the three weeks that the Bank paid in specie, its payments amounted to about five millions six hundred and thirty thousand dollars, viz. :

Bonds of Planters Bank,	240,000
To individual depositors. only	176,000
To State banks.	1,044,000
And, redemption of bank notes	4,170,000

Of this last item, one million and a half were for notes in the hands of the other banks of Philadelphia beyond the five millions included in the agreement; five hundred thousand for post notes over-due, and eleven hundred thousand for accumulated notes which had been protested and sued for. The drain, instead of being extraordinary, and such as could not have been anticipated, was in reality less than, under all the circumstances of the case, might have been expected.

In the preceding sketch, the acts of the Bank have been considered only in reference to their effect on the currency of the country. It may be affirmed that, in this respect, that bank, subsequent to the first general suspension of May 1837, has been the principal, if not the sole, cause of the delay in resuming, and of the subsequent suspensions. In every respect it has been a public nuisance. The original error consisted in the ambitious attempt to control and direct the commerce of the country; in the arrogant assumption of a pretended right to decide on the expediency of performing that which was an absolute duty; and in a manifest and deliberate deviation from the acknowledged principles of sound and legitimate banking.

It is not intended here to investigate the facts of a more culpable nature which are laid to the charge of the administrators of the Bank. The application of nine hundred thousand dollars secret service money, should be made public. The mismanagement and gross neglect, which could in a few years devour two-thirds of a capital of thirty-five millions, are incomprehensible, and have no parallel in the history of banks. The catastrophe has had an injurious effect abroad on the securities of the several States,

---

Bank, of sustaining specie payments now that confidence was entirely lost. The writer added that, if the other Philadelphia banks would discard that of the United States and resume alone, not one, but three millions ought to be advanced for that purpose by the banks of the city of New York.

impaired commercial credit, and shaken confidence between man
and man. It is natural that the shareholders, so deeply injured,
should cling to the hope of preserving the institution, and of thus
partly repairing their losses. Every facility consistent with the
public good should be granted, every forbearance practised, every delay allowed, which may enable them to save the remnants
of the wreck. But it is due to the moral feeling of the country,
not less than to the security of its fiscal concerns, that this disgraced and dangerous corporation should not be permitted any
longer to exist. How, after so many violations of its charter, its
existence has been so long protracted, is indeed unintelligible!

REMEDIES.

STATE LEGISLATION.

It can hardly be expected that twenty-six independent States
should all adopt such systems of legislation, as may secure a
sound and uniform currency. But there are some great centres
of commerce, which necessarily control the banking operations
of the greater part of the country. In the present course of
trade, the great importing sea-ports are generally creditor places;
and the principal centres alluded to will be found to be, Boston,
New-York, Philadelphia and Baltimore, Charleston, and New-
Orleans. Providence, on account of its manufactures, Savannah
and Mobile, on the sea-coast, Cincinnati, Louisville, and St.
Louis, in the interior, are the next most important points. Some
approximation of the relative importance of the great centres
may be derived from the aggregate of the foreign imports
and of the exports of each of them respectively. Supposing
the whole to consist of one hundred parts, Boston has about
twelve, New-York *forty-seven*, Philadelphia and Baltimore *fourteen*, Charleston and Savannah *seven*, New-Orleans and Mobile

twenty. The influence of domestic manufactures, of mines, and of other considerations, must of course vary the result.

Of those great centres, the two first are secure ; and Charleston appears to have adopted a correct course. The banking system of New-Orleans is founded on principles so different from those of the Atlantic States, particularly in reference to the large amount loaned on real estate security, that it is difficult to form a correct opinion of it. But the elements of wealth are so great, and the interest of sustaining a sound currency so obvious, that, notwithstanding the embarrassed situation of the adjacent States, great hopes are entertained of an ultimate favorable result in that quarter. Under all the circumstances of our present situation, it seems that, provided a correct course should be adopted by the banks of Philadelphia, and by the Legislature of Pennsylvania, an early and nearly general resumption of specie payments would naturally take place.

The first step that appears absolutely necessary does not apply to Pennsylvania alone. All the States which have incurred debts, and which have not yet adopted efficient measures in that respect, must provide for the punctual payment of the interest and the gradual extinguishment of their debt. This must be done by providing an actual revenue, by taxes whenever necessary, and not by any new loans, or any other temporary expedient. The States must rely on their own resources, neither on any direct or indirect assumption of State debts by the General Government, nor on any assistance to be derived from the banks : neither must the banks depend on the aid of the States for carrying on their operations. The difficulties are greater in some States than in others. A great error has been committed by those which have advanced their credit for the especial purpose of establishing banks, in places where a very moderate banking capital was sufficient for all legitimate purposes. Sanguine expectations have induced others to undertake premature, and far too extensive, internal improvements, which, in their unfinished state, are nearly or altogether unproductive. The honor and interest of every State require, and justice demands, that its credit should be restored. Public and private credit are intimately connected. That of individuals is impaired when public faith is not preserved. A resumption of specie payments, on the part of banks and of individuals, will at once inspire a greater confidence in the stocks of the States where it may take place. There is none whose resources are not adequate to the object in view.

Philadelphia had a sound capital, greater in proportion to its commerce than that of New-York, or of almost any other city in the Union; its banks proper were sound and cautiously administered: not one of them had ever failed. But they have for several years been pressed by two great evils, the United States Bank and the State Legislature. They have at last got rid of the first burthen, from which they ought to have detached themselves long ago. Their available means are undoubtedly impaired by the efforts they made to sustain the Great Bank, and by the debt due to them on that account. Still, provided they are sustained by the commercial community and by public opinion, and provided the State Legislature ceases to oppress them under color of granting them relief, there does not seem to be any real obstacle to their soon resuming their former wonted and honorable situation.

The suspension of specie payments of October 1839, was legalized by the Legislature of Pennsylvania, on condition that the banks, thus indulged, should make certain loans of money to the State, and resume their payments in January 1841. To take from them their most available resources, had a direct tendency to put it out of their power to resume their payments within the prescribed time. Those resources, which should have been applied to the reduction of the liabilities of the banks, and to the measures necessary for a resumption, were diverted from their legitimate object, in order to defray the annual expenditures, or to pay the interest on the debt of the State.

The two last General Assemblies of Pennsylvania have, however, adopted efficient measures to arrest the progress of the debt, and to provide for the payment of the interest. A new annual revenue, derived from taxation alone, and which is expected, according to the most correct estimates, not to fall short of two millions two hundred thousand dollars, is specifically pledged to the maintenance of the public credit; and the interest on the public debt cannot exceed two millions, and will probably fall short of that sum. The ordinary expenses of Government, and the repairs of the public works, appear to be nearly, if not altogether, provided for by the tolls and other revenues of the State. Thus far, great praise is due to the Legislature for having extricated the State from the difficulties in which it had been involved, and for having fearlessly resorted to those direct means which alone could effect the purpose.

After having accomplished the principal object, nothing else remained than to provide for the payment of arrears, and the ordinary annual expenditures of the current year, amounting together to three millions one hundred thousand dollars. It is deeply to be lamented that, instead of also pursuing the simplest and most direct course for this object, the Legislature should have resorted to a novel, complex, and most condemnable plan.

A loan for the sum thus wanted is authorised, for which a five per cent. stock will be issued, to be redeemed at the end of five years, or earlier at the pleasure of the Legislature. To that loan, certain banks (*l*) are alone authorised to subscribe, to an amount bearing, according to their respective capitals, a ratio varying from eight to twenty-five per cent. to the capital. And, on paying into the State Treasury the amount subscribed in their bank notes of one, two and five dollars, they are credited on the Treasury books for an equal amount of the stock.

The notes thus issued are payable only in the same stock, and in the following manner. The holder of the notes to an amount of one hundred dollars, on surrendering the same to the issuing bank, receives an order on the Auditor General for a certificate of an equal amount of the stock, and the notes surrendered are cancelled. The State, until the notes are thus redeemed, pays to the banks interest, at the rate of one per cent. a year, on the stock for which they are credited on the Treasury books. And after the notes have been thus redeemed and funded, the State pays, through the agency of the banks, the interest of five per cent. to the holders of the stock which has been issued in payment of the notes. That interest is paid out of the proceeds of the tax on bank dividends; and if this should not be sufficient, the deficiency is paid out of the revenue provided by the act.

All the notes issued under the provisions of. the act, are

(*l*) Viz., as appears from the subsequent provisions, those banks which are subject to a tax on their dividends.

receivable for debts due to the commonwealth and to the issuing banks respectively, and also on deposit, by the said banks respectively, payable in like currency, special contracts for deposits excepted. All the notes may be re-issued from the Treasury and from the issuing banks respectively; and the banks generally may receive and issue any of the notes created by the act.

All the banks, except that of the United States, which own any portion of the funded debt of the State, may, on transferring the same as security to the Auditor General, issue notes to an equal amount, of the same denomination, and receivable and redeemable in the same manner as the notes before described. But the banks which are exempted from a tax on their dividends shall not issue a greater amount of notes, than in the aforesaid ratio to their respective capitals; and the banks subject to that tax shall not, under this section of the act, issue a greater amount than seven per cent. of their respective capitals. The interest on the stock thus transferred is suspended, during the time the said stock remains in the hands of the Auditor General (m).

17th Sect. No bank, which shall comply with the provisions of this act, shall be subject, by way of penalty or otherwise, to a greater rate of interest than six per cent. per annum. The resolution of April 1840, which provided for the resumption of specie payments, is repealed. And all the provisions of any act of incorporation, or of any law of the State, which provided for the forfeiture of any charter, by reason of the non-payment of any of the liabilities of the bank, or which prohibited the banks from making loans and discounts, issuing their own notes, or declaring dividends during the suspension of specie payments, are suspended, until further legislative action, *and* until the. Legislature shall provide for the repayment of the loan of three millions one hundred thousand dollars authorised by the act. But the dividends are limited to five per cent. during the suspension.

(m) It appears, therefore, that all the banks, whether subject to, or exempt from a tax on their dividends, are authorised to issue notes in the ratio to their capitals fixed by the law; and that, in addition thereto, the banks subject to that tax may issue notes to an amount not exceeding seven per cent. of their capital.

The banks subject to a tax on their dividends, which shall not take their due proportion of the loan, according to the ratio fixed by law, (not including, it seems, the seven per cent. additional which appears to be optional,) and the other banks, which shall not deposit at least five per cent. on their capitals respectively, shall remain subject to the provisions of the laws now in force, and be excepted from the benefit of the provisions of the 17th section of the act. Nor shall the United States Bank be entitled to the said benefits, unless the stockholders consent to be subject to any general laws to be *hereafter* passed for the regulation of the banks of the commonwealth. There are other provisions authorising and facilitating the dissolution and liquidation of that bank, with the consent of the stockholders.

The residue of the act provides for raising an additional revenue, and for appropriating the proceeds of the loan of three millions one hundred thousand dollars, viz. about two millions two hundred thousand for repairs and arrears on account of the internal improvements, and about eight hundred thousand for schools and the other ordinary annual expenses of Government. Those objects were evidently blended in the same law with the provisions respecting the banks, in order to ensure the adoption of these provisions.

Viewed simply as a fiscal operation, it makes the banks only the agents of the State. They sign the notes *pro forma*, and redeem them in its behalf. The State puts the notes in circulation, uses them for its own benefit, redeems them with its own stock, pays the interest, and is bound at the end of five years to pay the principal, in specie, with its own funds. The banks, for their agency, receive the compensation of one per cent. a year on the notes, so long as they remain in circulation. The notes are substantially an emission of bills of credit, by the State and for the use of the State. How far this operation may in itself be proper, or consistent with the Constitution of the United States, are questions which do not come within the scope of this essay. The measure, considered only in reference to its effect on the currency and on the resumption of specie payments, hardly requires to be discussed. It is almost sufficient to have stated the provisions of the law.

The banks of Philadelphia, notwithstanding the difficulties

which they had to encounter, had succeeded in keeping their currency, their deposits, their liabilities payable on demand, all which is generally called " Philadelphia funds," at a discount, compared with specie, of less than five per cent. An emission of a new species of currency is now authorised, which, being only a promise to issue a State stock to the same amount, is, on the day when it is issued, worth intrinsically no more than that stock, or less than eighty per cent. of its nominal value. It may be, that the demand created by having made that currency receivable in payment of debts to the commonwealth and to the bank, may enhance that value. This is altogether conjectural: and it cannot certainly be expected that it will become equal to that of the actual currency at this moment of the Philadelphia banks. Under the most favorable aspect, it is still a legalized emission of a depreciated, fluctuating and irredeemable paper, analogous to a falsification of the legal coin of the country. And in order to carry this plan into effect, it has been deemed necessary to compel the banks to receive that paper in payment of the debts due to them, and to give a solemn legislative sanction to a protracted suspension of specie payments ; that is to say, to a continued immoral and illegal violation of engagements and contracts, for a term which may be not less than five years.

Had there been no other object in view, than that of providing for the discharge of the arrears and necessary expenses of the year, for which a loan was indispensable, the simple and direct course was to borrow the money on the best terms on which it could be obtained. This is the cheapest and wisest, as it is the most honest mode. Every other complex, and, as it is called, ingenious contrivance is nothing but quackery, if not something worse. There is indeed much difficulty, when heavy taxes become necessary, in selecting those which will be most equal and productive, least oppressive and arbitrary. But there is no more mystery in directing, in ordinary times, the finances of a nation, than in arranging the fiscal concerns of a commercial house. In both cases, if it becomes necessary to borrow, you must pay for the money, according to its market price, and to the credit of the borrower. Indeed, in that respect, the State has the advantage of not being trammelled by its own absurd usury laws, which may compel the individual to pay a dearer price for the loan than he otherwise would.

In the year 1798, the United States borrowed five millions at eight per cent. per annum. During the last war, they gave their six per cent. stock for money, at the rate of eighty per cent. of its nominal value. Which was the most eligible mode is a debatable question. But, on both occasions, they were obliged to give, and gave without hesitation, their stock for the highest price it could command. It is what every Government, which has any regard for its credit, always does. The State of New York wanted also three millions of dollars for the service of this year. The market price of her stocks is higher than that of those of Pennsylvania. Yet she did not attempt to borrow at five per cent., but has authorised a *voluntary* loan at the rate of six per cent. It is probable that a similar stock, issued by Pennsylvania, could not, at this moment, have been negotiated at par. But, with the knowledge that efficient provision had been made for the payment of the interest of the public debt, and that a course of measures had been adopted which would prevent its increase, had the Legislature only taken measures for hastening, instead of protracting, the resumption of specie payments, the effect on the public credit of the State would have been immediate; and a direct loan at six per cent. might have been negotiated on favorable terms.

There is, indeed, no other remedy, so far as it depends on the State, for the evils inflicted by the act of the late General Assembly. For, if the banks accept the proposal, they may claim, as a condition of the contract, that all the suspending clauses of the act shall continue in force, until provision shall have been made for the re-payment of the loan. This cannot be done otherwise than by negotiating a money loan in the ordinary way. Whether this shall be done by the next Legislature, depends on the will of the people. At this time, and had it not been for that most unfortunate impediment, there would have been no more difficulty in resuming specie payments in Philadelphia within sixty days, provided the commercial community of that city required it, than there is now in sustaining those payments in New York. New England and New York should, at all times, give every possible aid in promoting that object. It is a national concern, on account both of the importance of that city, and of its great influence over the commercial transactions and currency of the West and of the South.

The dangers of a paper currency are such, that it becomes necessary to inquire whether the banking system adopted, in those States where the result has been most favorable, may not be susceptible of improvement. For that purpose the laws which govern the banks of New York will now be examined. They are better known to the writer than those of any other State; the system has been at least as successful here as in any other part of the Union; and it now embraces both restricted chartered banks, and free banking associations established under a general law.

The various legal provisions, by which the banks of the State of New York are governed, consist principally of general laws respecting monied corporations, partly of clauses inserted in the several charters and nearly the same in all, but which it would have been better to have included amongst the general laws.

The privileges granted by the charters are, 1st, the Act of Incorporation itself, which enables the bank to contract, to sue and be sued, and generally to act, in reference to the object for which it is incorporated, in the same manner as might be done by a natural person; 2dly, the limitation of responsibility to the capital of the bank, thus rendering the shareholders irresponsible in their personal capacity; 3dly, the monopoly, till lately, of carrying on banking operations.

Those operations are not expressly defined by the general laws of the land, but by the charters themselves, and substantially as follows, viz.: that the bank shall have power to carry on the business of banking, by discounting bills, notes, and other evidences of debt; by receiving deposits; by buying and selling gold and silver bullion, foreign coins, and bills of exchange; by issuing bills, notes, and other evidences of debt; and by exercising such other incidental powers as shall be necessary to carry on such business.

It might be inferred by implication, that the banks could not legally carry on any other species of business. For greater security, it is further expressly provided in all the charters: 1st, that no bank shall hold any real estate but such as is requisite for its immediate accommodation, or such as may be mortgaged, conveyed or purchased in satisfaction of debts, or for the purpose of securing debts; 2dly, that it shall not, directly or indirectly, deal or trade in buying or selling any goods, wares, merchandizes, or commodities whatsoever, or in buying or selling any stock created under any act of the United States, or of any particular State, unless in selling the same when truly pledged, by way of security, for debts due to the said corporation.

The location, duration, and capital of each bank respectively, are also determined by its charter. The other provisions refer to the following objects, viz. :

1. *Capital.*—No bank can commence its operations until the whole of its capital has been paid in specie or current bank bills ; nor until an affidavit to that effect, and stating that no stockholder has paid any part of his shares by a discounted note, or directly or indirectly with any loan from the bank, has been made by the President and Cashier of the bank and filed with the Comptroller. False swearing in that respect is deemed perjury, and punished as such.

For the purpose of preserving the capital, the banks are forbidden, besides other provisions, to make any dividend except from their surplus profits. In calculating the profits, all the expenses, the interest due on debts contracted by the bank, and all the losses, including therein all the debts due to the bank on which no interest has been paid for one year, must be deducted ; and if the amount of losses should exceed that of the profits then possessed, the deficiency must be charged as a reduction of the capital ; and no dividends can be paid until the deficit of the original capital shall be made good. That capital cannot be reduced without leave of the Legislature.

2. *Restrictions on Banking Operations.*—The banks are forbidden to have an amount of bank notes in circulation exceeding a rate which varies according to their respective capitals, so as not to exceed once and a half its amount when that capital is not more than one hundred thousand dollars, nor sixty

per cent. of that amount, when the capital is, or exceeds, two millions;. to extend their loans and discounts beyond twice and a half the amount of their respective capital; to issue notes not payable on demand, or bearing interest (post notes); to issue notes of a less denomination than one dollar; to purchase their notes for less than their nominal value; to lend or discount on the security of their own stock; to charge more than six per cent. interest on discounted notes payable within sixty-three days; to make, directly or indirectly, any loans or discounts to their directors respectively, to an amount exceeding in the aggregate one third of their capital.

3. *Directors.*—Besides the limitation on their own discounts, they are made personally liable, if consenting to any act in violation of the laws respecting monied corporations. Every director must have a number of shares determined by the charter. No director or officer of the bank is permitted to purchase, discount, or loan money on a note which has been rejected by the bank.

4. *Inspection and Publicity.*—It is the duty of three bank commissioners, appointed by the Governor and Senate, to inspect, once at least in every four months, the affairs of every bank; to examine all their books, papers, notes, bonds, and other evidences of debt; to ascertain the quantity of specie on hand, and generally the actual condition of the banks and their ability to fulfil their engagements. The commissioners are authorised to examine upon oath all the officers of the banks, or any other person, in relation to their affairs and condition; and they must report annually to the Legislature abstracts from the report made to them, and such other statements as they may deem useful.

5. *Suspension and Dissolution.*—All the banks created subsequent to the year 1828 are, by provisions inserted in their charters, directed, as has already been stated, to discontinue their operations, unless permitted by the Chancellor, if they shall neglect or refuse, for ten days, to redeem in specie any evidence of debt issued by them. This special provision has not been inserted in the charters of the old banks which have been renewed since that time. During a suspension of specie payments, the suspending banks are obliged to pay damages, at the

rate of ten per cent. a year, on every evidence of debt, the payment of which has been demanded and refused.

It is provided by the general laws, that, if any bank shall have lost one half of its capital stock, or shall have suspended the payment of its bills in specie for ninety days, or shall refuse to allow its officers to be examined upon oath by the commissioners, the said commissioners may, and, if they ascertain that the bank is insolvent, or has violated any of the provisions binding on such bank, they shall, apply to the Court of Chancery for an injunction against such bank and its officers. The Attorney General, and every creditor, director, and, in some cases, stockholder of the bank, may also apply for an injunction.

The Chancellor, upon any such application, may, according to circumstances, suspend or dismiss any of the officers of the bank, restrain it from exercising its corporate powers, sequestrate its property, dissolve it as an insolvent corporation, and appoint a receiver for the liquidation of its affairs.

It is further provided by the act of 3d December 1827, which sanctioned the first part of the Revised Statutes, that " the charter of every corporation, that shall thereafter be granted by the Legislature, shall be subject to alteration, suspension, and repeal, in the discretion of the Legislature" (n).

Finally, it is enacted by the third part of the Revised Statutes, passed as one act on the 10th December 1828, that " whenever any incorporated company shall have remained insolvent for one whole year; or for one year shall have neglected or refused to pay and discharge its notes or other evidences of debt; or for one year shall have suspended the ordinary and lawful business of such corporation; it shall be deemed to have surrendered the rights, privileges and franchises granted by any act of incorporation, or acquired under the laws of this State, and shall be adjudged to be dissolved" (o).

6. *Safety Fund.*—Every bank chartered, or the charter of which has been renewed subsequent to the act of April 2d 1829, pays annually, during six years, to the Treasurer of the State, a

---

(n) Revised Statutes, Part I., Chap. xviii., Title 3d, Section 8.

(o) Revised Statutes, Part III., Chap. viii., Title 4th, Art. 2d, Section 38.

sum equal to one half of one per cent. on its capital. These payments, called the "bank fund," are appropriated to the payment of such of the debts of any of the said banks which shall become insolvent, as shall remain unpaid, after applying the property and effects of such insolvent bank. And whenever the fund shall be reduced, by the payment of such debts, to less than three per cent. upon the aggregate capital of the banks, every bank shall again renew its annual payments of one-half of· one per cent. on its capital, until the fund shall again amount to three per cent. on the aggregate capital.

It cannot be denied that the banking system of the State of New York, since it has been subject to these regulations, has proved superior to most, and inferior to none, of the plans adopted in other States. The banks, though they did suspend, were the first to resume, and have ever since maintained specie payments. Since the year 1830, only two banks subject to the regulations, have been dissolved. One of these, having a capital of one hundred thousand dollars, was for some irregularity dissolved by act of the Legislature. It paid all its debts, and the whole of its capital to the stockholders. The other (the City Bank of Buffalo) was dissolved by process of law; and its entire capital of four hundred thousand dollars is sunk. During the same period of ten years, and under a regimen till lately much less severe, not less than nine banks in Boston, with a capital of three millions six hundred thousand dollars, have failed, or been dissolved; but in five of those cases, the creditors suffered no ultimate loss.

The provisions, which define and limit the legitimate operations of the banks, as well as those which ensure the actual payment of the capital, or are intended to preserve it entire, have proved efficient and do not seem to require any alteration. It has been often suggested, and instances have been adduced to prove, that provisions for ensuring the actual payment of capital might be evaded. The instances adduced have occurred when the provisions were inadequate. None has taken place amongst the New York banks subject to the present system. It will not be asserted that such instances may not occur; but when they are so extremely rare, to argue thence, that the provisions are unnecessary or inefficient, is as illogical as an attempt to prove that, because some criminals escape, laws for the punishment of crimes are unnecessary and inefficient.

For the enforcement of those provisions and of the other restrictions on banking operations, an inspection and thorough investigation of the affairs of the banks, by officers unconnected with those institutions, were necessary; and those investigations by the Bank Commissioners, as well as the publicity given to their statements, have proved eminently useful. No further provision in this respect seems necessary.

Two additional regulations only, of primary importance, will be suggested. The first relates to the restrictions on the amount of loans and discounts; the other to the provisions in case of suspension of specie payments.

The restriction on the amount of issues was originally almost nominal, inasmuch as it far exceeded the amount which any bank might or did issue. The amount now permitted is still too great, at least for banks which have but a small capital. This condition may still be retained; but it will lose much of its importance, provided the restriction upon the loans and discounts shall be modified.

All the debits and credits of a bank may, for the sake of perspicuity, be reduced, on the one side, to the capital, circulation and deposites; on the other, to the real estate, the amount of loans, discounts, and other investments bearing interest, and the specie. For all the other items, of which the principal are the notes of other banks on hand, and the balances due to and from other banks, may be included under some of the general heads above mentioned. Thus, for instance, all the balances due to other banks are deposits; and all the notes of other banks, or balances due by them, should, if the bank has been properly administered, be available resources, tantamount to specie. It is obvious, that the maximum of the investments bearing interest will regulate all the other varying items.

Supposing, for instance, that the maximum of discounts, loans, and other investments, bearing interest, should never exceed once and three-fifths of the capital of the bank, and that the statement of a bank, having a capital of one million, should on any given day be as follows, viz.:

Capital.....................$1,000,000	Real estate.....................$ 100,000
Circulation and deposits.... 1,000,000	Loans, discounts, stocks, &c. 1,600,000
	Specie.......................... 300,000
2,000,000	2,000,000

—it is evident that, since the capital and real estate are constant quantities, and the amount of loans, &c. is at its maximum, any increase in the circulation and deposits, or any other liabilities of the bank, must necessarily produce a corresponding increase of specie or available resources of the bank. And the effect of this would be to strengthen instead of weakening the bank; since the ratio of available resources to liabilities payable on demand would thereby be increased. The efficiency of the provision depends entirely on the reduction of the maximum of loans and discounts, so that they shall not exceed the amount necessary to ensure a sufficient dividend.

That maximum is now fixed at twice and a half the amount of the capital, which would yield a gross profit of at least fifteen per cent.; and, after deducting three per cent. for expenses, tax, and contingencies, leave a dividend of twelve per cent. on the capital; and a dividend of even fifteen per cent. has accordingly been sometimes realized by country banks with a small capital. Considered as a whole, the excessive and fatal expansions of the years 1836–1837, could not have taken place, had the maximum been properly regulated. On the 1st of January 1837, the loans, discounts and stocks of the ninety banks subject to the bank-fund law, and having a capital of thirty-two millions five hundred thousand dollars, amounted to sixty-nine millions, that is to say, to twice and one-eighth of their capital. The consequence was, an amount of circulation and deposits of forty-five millions, with less than six millions in specie (p).

As the legal interest of New-York is seven per cent., the average interest on discounts may, independent of occasional profits on exchange, be estimated at six and a half per cent. If, therefore, the maximum of loans, discounts, and all other investments

(p) The Manhattan Company, which was not subject to the law, with a capital of $2,050,000, had extended its loans and discounts to $5,450,000; and its circulation and deposits amounted to $4,920,000.

bearing interest, was reduced to once and a half the amount of the capital, the gross profits would amount to nine and three quarters per cent., and, after deducting three per cent. for expenses, &c. leave a dividend of six and three quarters per cent. on the capital. In point of fact, a reference to the numerous bank statements of different States, which have been lately published, will show, that the average amount of the loans, discounts, &c. of well-administered banks, is nearly in that ratio.

On the 1st January 1840, the loans, discounts and stocks of the ninety banks of the State of New-York, subject to the bank-fund law, and having a capital of thirty-two millions five hundred and fifty thousand dollars, amounted to fifty-three millions four hundred and twenty thousand dollars, that is to say, in the ratio of *one hundred and sixty-four* to *one hundred* of their capital. The capital of the eighteen city banks, of the same description, amounted to sixteen millions six hundred thousand dollars, and their loans, discounts and stocks to twenty-five millions and forty thousand dollars, that is to say, in the ratio of *one hundred and fifty-one* to *one hundred* of their capital. The aggregate dividend of the eighteen city banks was 6.87 per cent., and that of the seventy-two country banks 8.82 per cent. on their capital. The great importance and practicability of a provision fixing that maximum are obvious. The ratio, at most, of *one hundred and sixty* to *one hundred* of the capital may be proper, as, under that, banks will hardly ever exceed *one hundred and fifty* to *one hundred.*

With respect to suspensions, the provision which compels all the new banks to discontinue their operations, except the securing and collecting of debts, whenever they shall decline for ten days to redeem in specie any evidence of debt issued by such banks respectively, should, in the first place, be expressly extended to all their liabilities payable on demand, and be made applicable to all the banks without exception.

This being done, and in case the Chancellor should permit any bank thus suspended to proceed in its business, the alteration proposed is that, notwithstanding the leave thus given, the bank should, until it had resumed payments in specie, be prohibited to issue any of its notes, to increase the aggregate of its loans and discounts, or to increase the amount of loans previously obtained by any of its officers or directors. For the purpose of rendering the first of these provisions efficient, it would be further necessary to prohibit any bank whatever to issue the notes of any bank which had suspended specie payments. The following advantages would ensue.

In the first place, it is a natural remedy. Since the banks have been permitted to issue a paper currency on the express condition of its being at all times redeemable in specie, the permission should cease whenever the condition is not performed. The prohibition would also have a direct tendency to enable the solvent banks to resume within a short time. And finally, it would make it the interest of all the parties immediately concerned, and of the whole community, to prevent a suspension, or to make it of the shortest possible duration.

Experience has shown, that persons laboring under embarrassments, or from some temporary, selfish or erroneous motives, may promote, or protract, a general suspension. If they are made certain, that such a measure will make money more scarce, as it is called, instead of more abundant, and that their situation will be worse instead of being improved, one of the causes which most seriously endangers the banking system will be removed.

Other improvements of less importance might be suggested.

The amount discounted for any one director might be limited; the banks might be prohibited from making any loans to the president or cashier; and these two officers should not be permitted to deal in stocks.

The annual tax of one half per cent., imposed under the name of "safety fund," is unjust towards the banks which are well administered, and injurious to the community at large. To make a bank responsible for the misconduct of another, sometimes very distant, and over which it has no control, is a premium given to neglect of duty and to mismanagement, at the expense of the banks which have performed their duty and been cautiously administered. That provision gives a false credit to some institutions, which, not enjoying perfect confidence, would not otherwise be enabled to keep in circulation the same amount of notes; and it therefore has a tendency unnecessarily to increase the amount of paper money. The fund would be inadequate in case of any great failure; and it provides at best only against ultimate loss, and not at all against the danger of a general suspension.

It has been suggested that, although every legislative attempt to make a paper currency payable at different places, a general and uniform currency for an extensive country, is improper and must fail (q), yet the safety fund tax might be rendered less improper, by applying it to each county, or other district of country prescribed by law, respectively. Thus the banks would each be made responsible, to the extent of the tax, for the banks only within the same county or district. They would all thereby be induced to watch and regulate those in their own vicinity.

In connexion with this branch of the subject, there is a measure which, though belonging to the administration of banks rather than to legal enactments, is suggested on account of its great importance. Few regulations would be more useful, in preventing dangerous expansions of discounts and issues on the part of the city banks, than a regular exchange of notes and checks, and an actual daily or semi-weekly payment of the balances. It must be recollected, that it is by this process alone that a Bank of the United States has ever acted, or been supposed to act, as a regulator of the currency. Its action would not, in that respect, be wanted in any city, the banks of which would, by adopting the process, regulate themselves. It is one of the principal ingredients of the system of the banks of Scotland. The bankers of London, by the daily exchange of drafts at the clearing-house, reduce the ultimate balance to a very small sum; and that balance is immediately paid in notes of the Bank of England. The want of a similar arrangement amongst the banks of this city produces relaxation, favors improper expansions, and is attended with serious inconveniences. The principal difficulty in the way of an arrangement for that purpose, is the want of a common medium other than specie for effecting the payment of balances. These are daily fluctuating; and a perpetual drawing and redrawing of specie from and into the Banks is unpopular and inconvenient.

(q) This subject will again be adverted to in reference to a Bank of the United States.

In order to remedy this, it has been suggested, that a general *cash office* might be established, in which each bank should place a sum in specie, proportionate to its capital, which would be carried to its credit in the books of the office. Each bank would be daily debited or credited in those books for the balance of its account with all the other banks. Each bank might at any time draw for specie on the office for the excess of its credit beyond its quota; and each bank should be obliged to replenish its quota, whenever it was diminished one half, or in any other proportion agreed on.

It may be, that some similar arrangement might be made in every other county, or larger convenient district, of the State. It would not be necessary to establish there a general cash office. Each of the banks of Scotland has an agent at Edinburgh, and the balances are there settled twice a week, and paid generally by drafts on London. In the same manner the balances due by the banks, in each district, might be paid by drafts on New York, or any other place agreed on; and the notes of the several banks in the same district would be received by all, and be a common and uniform currency for the whole district. But the process, which is practicable for a country of no greater extent than that portion of Scotland where banks are established, cannot be extended beyond certain limits. It cannot certainly be applied to the whole of the United States, nor, it is believed, to the whole State of New York, so as to make the notes issued by all the banks a uniform currency for the whole.

Paper money is from its nature a local currency, confined to the place where it is made payable and to its vicinity. The selection of the place or places where it is made payable may be left to each bank respectively; but they should not be compelled by law to make it payable or redeemable at more than one place. In order to obviate this difficulty, the country banks of the State of New York have been enjoined, by a late law, to redeem their notes at New York or Albany, at a certain fixed discount. This is, in fact, an attempt to regulate the rate of exchange; which is not a proper object for legislation, and should be left to be regulated by the course of trade.

Although the former general laws prohibited only notes

under one dollar, a subsequent act did, for a short time, extend the prohibition to all notes under five dollars. This is in itself a proper measure; inasmuch as it lessens the gross amount of issues; contributes, as far as it goes, in making the wages of labor and the articles of consumption which are daily retailed, payable only in specie; and protects the poor classes of the community against the contingency of a depreciated currency. The prohibition would be still more useful and efficient, if it could be extended to all notes under twenty dollars. But there has been a universal demand for notes under five dollars, not only in this, but in many other States; and the issue of notes of that description has again been permitted by a law of this State.

It is believed that this demand may be principally ascribed to the act of Congress, which has rated silver under its true value as compared with gold. It seems to be at all times improper to give a legal relative value to the two precious metals, different from their respective market price. This indeed varies according to the variations, in the respective demand and supply in different countries. But these variations are small, and an average ratio may be assumed sufficiently correct for all practical purposes during a number of years. If a contrary course be pursued, the precious metal which is underrated will cease to circulate freely, and will become a merchandise. It may also be observed, as regards the United States, that gold is imported from countries where it is not produced, and can therefore be naturally imported only when exchanges are favorable; whilst silver is imported directly from Mexico and other parts of America, of which it is the natural annual product, and must, as the cotton of the United States, be necessarily exported annually, without regard to price or rate of exchange. Before the act of Congress alluded to, the silver crop of Mexico did naturally flow into the United States; it now seeks the more favorable market of England.

But the immediate effect of that act on the currency of the country, has been to give to the silver, necessary for change or small payments, a legal nominal value less than its actual worth. It is believed that a similar experiment had never before been attempted in any country. Everywhere else, as well as in America, the silver coins, daily wanted for exchange, had been

9

made either to correspond, or to be inferior in value, to gold coins, or to silver coins of a higher denomination. The necessary result is to drive silver from circulation; and that inconvenience has been in part obviated, only by permitting small foreign silver coins, though depreciated from five to ten per cent., to pass at their nominal value. Hence, the demand for notes of one and two dollars was so urgent, that foreign notes of that denomination became a general circulating medium, in open violation of the laws of this State. To permit its banks to issue small notes, became in fact a measure necessary, in order to protect the community against a worse description of paper.

There seem to be but two remedies for that evil, and they depend on the action of Congress. The first, and, it is believed, the most proper, would be to alter the ratio of gold to silver, according to their true relative value. This would render a new gold coinage necessary, and might cost about three hundred thousand dollars, in order to redeem the existing coinage at its nominal value. The other mode would be, to adopt the British plan, and to issue as tokens, not as a legal tender, but as a voluntary currency, a silver coinage depreciated by alloy five to ten per cent. In that case the coinage must, like that of copper coins, be made by Government, and not for individuals; and it is necessary, in order to prevent any excess beyond the amount actually requisite for the wants of the community, that the Mint should at all times, when required, redeem such coinage at its nominal value.

According to a return made to the State's Senate, the amount of the different denominations of the notes issued by the several banks of this State was on the 1st of January 1836, as follows:

Under five dollars	$2,589,714
Of five do.	6,029,933
Of ten and twenty	5,687,004
Of fifty and one hundred	3,131,175
Of above one hundred	3,451,100
	$20,888,926

The country banks had in circulation only twenty-five thousand dollars in notes of a higher denomination than one hundred dollars.

FREE BANKING.

Notwithstanding the comparatively favorable result of the New York restrictive system of chartered banks, it has been strenuously assailed; and the attempt has been made to substitute for it that which has been called *free banking*.

A monopoly, embracing all the ordinary banking operations, had in this State been created in favor of the chartered banks. By an act passed in 1818 and confirmed, as included in the first part of the Revised Statutes, by the act of December 3d, 1827, it was enacted that, "no person, association of persons or body corporate, except such bodies corporate as are expressly authorised by law, (the chartered banks,) shall keep any office for the purpose of receiving deposits, or discounting notes or bills, or issuing any evidences of debt, to be loaned, or put in circulation as money; nor shall they issue any bills or promissory notes or evidences of debt as private bankers, for the purpose of loaning them, or putting them in circulation as money, unless thereto specially authorised by law."

So much of that law as forbade any person or association of persons to keep offices for the purpose of receiving deposits or discounting notes or bills, was repealed by a law passed February 4th, 1837 (*q*). It is not believed that any such prohibition, that of receiving deposits or discounting notes or bills, has ever existed in any of the other States, or in any other country. It was denounced by the writer of this essay more than ten years ago. And it must be well understood, that, in the discussion respecting free banking, the only question at issue relates exclusively to the power of substituting bank notes, or paper money, for a specie currency. It is now universally agreed, that with that single exception, every other species of banking operations, not only must be open to all, but requires no more restrictions than any other species of commerce.

(*q*) But any corporation, created by the laws of any other State or country, is still forbidden to keep any office for the purpose of receiving deposits, discounting notes or bills, or issuing bank notes.

The term "free banking," or, to speak more correctly, free issuing of paper money, embraces two distinct propositions; first, that all persons, or associations of persons, should be permitted to issue paper money on the same terms; secondly, that paper money may be issued by all persons, or associations, without any legislative restrictions.

The exclusive right of issuing a paper currency, granted to the chartered banks, was a monopoly; and monopolies can never exist without violating, to a certain extent, individual rights. But the actual evils produced by that particular monopoly have been greatly exaggerated, and should be reduced to their true value.

The right of issuing paper money as currency, like that of issuing gold and silver coins, belongs exclusively to the nation, and cannot be claimed by any individuals. If it be insisted that Government has no right to part with it, unless it be granted to all, it must be recollected that a right which from its nature cannot be exercised by an individual, is for him a nullity. The right in question can be exercised only by men of wealth, or by impostors. The poor classes cannot enjoy it: the right claimed is only, that all wealthy persons should be placed on an equal footing.

The monopoly also is in that case limited to the formation of the banks. The favored or original subscribers expect to make a profit of about five per cent. upon their shares; and thus far the monopoly extends. From the moment the bank has been organised, the monopoly ceases; every person may participate and become an associate in the banking business who can purchase bank shares; and these, being generally of twenty-five or fifty dollars each, are within the reach of almost all the sober and industrious members of the community.

Competition amongst the monopolists had also rendered the privilege valueless. There is not a single city bank, chartered subsequent to the year 1833, the stock of which is not below par. The small profit anticipated by the original subscribers has not been realised. On the other hand, the partiality exhibited by the Legislature in granting charters, had prevented any immoderate increase of the banking capital of this city, and that was a beneficial result; for the permission of issuing paper money, when given to all, has a tendency to increase its quantity, and the dangers to which such issues are always liable.

The opposition to the banking system was originally, in this State, as much against paper currency, by whomsoever issued, as against the monopoly enjoyed by the banks; and the preceding observations have been introduced principally because, in pursuing too eagerly that which was almost a shadow, the opponents seem to have lost sight of the principal object, and to have remained satisfied that there should be a dangerous excess of paper money, provided every body should be permitted to issue it.

But, even if it should be satisfactorily proved that the monopoly of chartered banks has been attended with favorable results as regards the soundness of the currency, the dangers of special, substituted for general, legislation are a paramount objection. The very essence of law consists in its being equal and general; and, although there are some necessary exceptions, special legislation should never be resorted to whenever it can possibly be avoided.

The danger of special laws is greatest when they relate to monied institutions, or to special appropriations of money. It is generally believed, that the original charters of some of the city banks were, about thirty years ago, obtained by direct corruption. Although, in latter years, nothing more has been alleged against the Legislature than the influence of party spirit, or yielding to personal solicitations, yet the danger, and even the suspicion, of being controlled by more degrading motives should be avoided. The fatal consequences of the baneful influence of the banking interest in other States are but too well known. In the case now under consideration, it is believed that a general law may be substituted for special legislation. The principal object will be obtained, provided the law be equal, that is to say, provided that all may be permitted to issue a paper currency on the same terms. But it is at the same time the firm conviction of the writer, that it is necessary, in order to secure a sound currency, that restrictions should be imposed upon all those who do issue the paper.

The proposition, that a paper currency may be issued by all, without any legislative restrictions, appears to be founded on an erroneous application of the principle of free trade. Free competition, in producing or dealing in any commodity, causes a reduction in the cost, or an improvement in the quality of the commodity. In money dealings, the same competition furnishes the use of money, and procures discounts of negotiable paper on the cheapest possible terms. But, issuing a paper currency is not dealing in money, but making money. The object, with respect to such currency, is not to produce a commodity cheaper, or varying in value, but, on the contrary, to furnish a substitute perfectly equal to gold or silver, and therefore of comparatively invariable value. Competition cannot make a cheaper currency, unless by making it worse than the legal coin of which it is the representative. In that case, it becomes analogous to a debased coin; and, if permitted to circulate, the bad generally drives away the faithful currency.

The general currency is always the standard of value of the country. To fix that standard, is as important and necessary as to fix the standard of weights and measures. Both are preliminary enactments which regulate and govern the freest possible trade. Gold and silver are the only standard of value recognised by the constitution. The power to regulate the value of gold and silver coins, as well as that of fixing the standard of weights and measures, is vested in the General Government. If any State Legislature permit the substitution of a paper for a gold or silver currency, it is bound so to regulate that currency, that it shall not alter the constitutional standard of value. The unrestricted right of coining gold or silver might be claimed with as much propriety as that of coining a paper currency.

No restrictions should be imposed on the acts of individuals, or associations, but such as are necessary to secure the rights of others, or to protect the whole community. But thus far the restrictions are proper and necessary. It will not be denied, that the evils of a depreciated currency, and those resulting from either the failure or the suspension of payment of those who issue a paper currency, universally fall most heavily on the poorer classes, and the most ignorant members of society. Restrictive laws are necessary for their immediate protection, as well as in order to guard against the general evils of an irredeemable currency.

It has been asserted, but not a single argument has been adduced in support of the assertion, that an indefinite number of unrestricted banking associations, or private bankers, would secure the community against the dangers of depreciation, suspension, or failure. If we appeal to experience, we find that the attempt to introduce that system in Michigan has been a complete failure, and has been the source of innumerable frauds. In some States, banks have been so unrestricted, and charters so liberally granted, that the result differed but little from complete free banking. Indeed, what more unrestrained system can be devised, than one which has produced nine hundred banks and branches, and, under which, all the restrictive laws are suspended in one half of the States. The evils under which we labor are principally due to the want of proper restriction upon the banks. The result has been favorable in proportion as the restraints have been most efficient.

Abroad, the privilege of issuing bank notes or private negotiable paper as currency, has nowhere, except in the British dominions, been considered as belonging of right to private individuals, or to joint stock associations. The experiment of free banking has been made only in Great Britain. With respect to the country bankers, the experiment may be considered as a failure. The number of bankruptcies and the amount of losses have been as great as under the former loose system of the banks of the several States; and, in proportion, far greater than in New York, under its better regulated system (r). The establishment of joint stock banking associations in England is of too recent a date, to form any definitive opinion of their eventual success. As yet, the example of the banks of Scotland can alone be appealed to in favor of free banking.

These banks cannot be compared to those of our large cities. They are, in fact, subordinate to the Bank of England; dependent for the payment of their balances on their London funds, hardly ever called on for specie, and suspending their specie payments

---

(r) The commissions of bankruptcy in England against bankers amounted to ninety-two during the years 1814–16; to sixty-five during the year 1825 and the three first months of 1826. The annual average was eight, from 1817 to 1824 inclusive.

whenever the Bank of England does suspend. But there must be a difference of habits between Scotland and even England, such as to have induced Parliament not to include the first in the general regulation which prohibits the issue of notes of a less denomination than five pounds. The difference is still greater between Scotland and America.

The spirit of enterprise will always be proportionate to its field, to the prospects open to it by the extent, geographical situation, and other circumstances of the country. The Scotch are an enterprising people; but the great and indeed extraordinary progress they have made in agriculture, manufactures and commerce, has been gradual and regular, obtained by persevering industry, and accompanied by a degree of prudent caution and of frugality altogether unknown in America. The population of Scotland is so far stationary, that it consists almost exclusively of natives of the land. The property, standing and character of every member of the commercial community are generally known. All persons may nominally establish banks; but their notes could not circulate unless received by the old banks; and these perfectly check each other by the regular payment of their respective balances. There is another ingredient, belonging to all the free banks of Great Britain, which will be immediately adverted to, and which would, it is believed, present an insurmountable obstacle to the introduction of unrestricted banks in America.

It would not be fair to draw general inferences against free banking, from the consequences of the defective system of New York. It will be perceived that the preceding observations have no reference to that system, and apply generally to the most perfect plan which might be devised. The provisions of the free banking act of New York will now be examined.

That law was passed in April 1838, at a time when the general prejudice against chartered banks, growing out of the warfare waged against them, had received additional strength from the suspension of specie payments, and when their monopoly was generally deprecated. Unfortunately no substitute, or rational plan of free banking, had been prepared by its advocates. The act bears internal evidence, that it was prepared by speculators, who took advantage of the opportunity for procuring a law that would suit their purpose.

There was, however, an intrinsic difficulty in passing a law founded on correct principles. The condition alluded to, as common to all private bankers who have ever been permitted to issue a paper currency, and to all the free banking associations of the same description which have ever existed, is the personal responsibility, to the whole extent of their fortune, of the private bankers and of all the shareholders in the banking associations. That responsibility is and has always been deemed essentially necessary. But whilst there were in existence ninety chartered banks spread over the whole State, whose shareholders were not subject to that responsibility, it would have been a mockery to authorise nominally free banks, with that responsibility attached to the associates. We may go farther, and say that such a plan would not be practicable, even if banks of a different description had not existed.

That degree of reciprocal confidence does not and cannot exist here, which would induce men of property to risk the whole of it, for the sake of obtaining the interest, or very little more than the ordinary interest, on their share in the association. That which is actually the fact in Scotland, is not practicable here. The laws, habits, and public opinion are not the same. American merchants, indeed, give large, and often indiscreet credits, but always in the expectation of a large profit. The shareholders of the Bank of Commerce, consisting of some of the most wealthy and respectable merchants and other men of capital of this city, aware of the greater confidence placed in chartered banks than in the new banking associations, have authorised the directors to accept a charter, if it could be obtained; but with the express condition, that it should not impose personal responsibility on the shareholders. No stronger proof can be given of the insurmountable reluctance to such a provision.

It is evident that some other guarantee is necessary, when there is no personal responsibility. That guarantee has heretofore always been that of the actual payment in specie of a capital fixed by law. This is the substitute which has always been required from the chartered banks, and which should have

10

been the essential condition imposed on the contemplated banking associations. The omission of any efficient provision for that purpose is the fundamental error of the law. It declares, indeed, that the capital shall not be less than one hundred thousand dollars, but does not specify of what that capital shall consist, nor when or how it shall be paid. The principal provisions of the act are the following.

The persons associated must file, in the office of the Secretary of State, a certificate specifying the name, place, duration, and capital of the association; and they may provide, by their articles of association, for an increase of their capital.

The banking business, which the associations may carry on, is defined nearly in the same words used in the charters of the old banks; and they are in the same manner forbidden to hold real estate otherwise than as is provided in the same charters.

No association shall, for the space of twenty days, have less than twelve and a half per cent. in specie on the amount of its circulation; nor, if its capital should be reduced, make dividends until the deficit shall have been made good; nor issue bank notes of a denomination less than one thousand dollars, payable at any other place than that where its business is carried on. By a subsequent amendment to the law, the associations are forbidden to issue post notes; and the provision respecting specie is repealed.

The associations shall pay damages at the rate of fourteen per cent. per annum, for non-payment only of every note in circulation, the payment of which shall have been demanded and refused.

The bank notes, which any association may issue, must be prepared and countersigned by the Comptroller of the State; and he is not to deliver to any association, notes to a greater amount than that of State stocks, or of mortgages, previously deposited with him by the associations respectively. The stocks, &c. thus deposited are pledged for securing the payment of the notes put in circulation, and shall be sold accordingly, whenever required for that purpose. By a subsequent law, mortgages and the stocks of the State alone are receivable.

Semi-annual statements of the affairs of every association,

verified by the oath of the president or cashier, must be transmitted to the Comptroller and published by him.

Upon the application of creditors or shareholders, the Chancellor may order a strict examination to be made of all the affairs of any association; and the result of such examination, together with his opinion thereon, shall be published in such manner as he may direct.

If any association shall neglect to transmit to the Comptroller the statements required, or if it shall have made dividends in violation of the provision above stated, or if it shall violate any of the provisions of the act, such association may be proceeded against and dissolved by the Court of Chancery.

The shares of the associations shall be transferable on their books; and every person, to whom such transfer shall be made, shall succeed to the rights and liabilities of prior shareholders. No shareholder shall be liable in his individual capacity for any contract or debt of the association, unless declared to be so liable by the articles of the association; and no association shall be dissolved by the death, or insanity, of any of the shareholders.

All contracts made and notes issued by any such association shall be signed by the president, or vice-president, and cashier. All suits, actions, and proceedings brought or prosecuted, in behalf of such association, may be brought or prosecuted in the name of the president; and all persons, having demands against the association, may maintain actions against the president. Such suits or actions shall not, in either case, abate by reason of the death, resignation, or removal from office of such president, but may be continued and prosecuted to judgment, in the name of, or against his successor in office, who shall exercise the powers and enjoy the rights of his predecessor.

All judgments and decrees rendered against such president, for any liability of the association, shall be enforced only against the joint property of the association. No change shall be made in the articles of association, by which the rights, remedies, or security of its existing creditors shall be weakened or impaired.

The original certificate filed with the Comptroller affords no security that the capital has been paid. It does not appear to require the sanction of an oath; and there is no penalty for making a false certificate. There is no provision, declaring of what the capital shall consist, or in what manner it shall be paid. The only provision, in that respect, is the obligation to deposit the stocks or mortgages, equal in amount to that of the bank notes issued by the association. Beyond that deposit, which by the supplementary law must amount to one hundred thousand dollars, no provision whatever is made for the residue of the capital. This may be nominal or real, consisting, at the will of the parties, of specie, mortgages or stocks of any description, of nominal debts, or of nothing at all. There is no provision to prevent the shareholders from paying their shares by giving their own notes. Even the minimum of securities deposited with the Comptroller, and intended as a guarantee for the payments of the issues, was not determined by the original law. An association depositing ten thousand or one thousand dollars, in stock of the most equivocal character, and announcing a capital of some millions of dollars that did not exist, was permitted to begin its operations. Heretofore, it had been deemed essential that the whole capital should be paid in specie. An honest institution, with a capital consisting of nothing but mortgages, has nothing to lend, and must necessarily begin its operations by contracting a debt. And those mortgages afford no available resources to meet the liabilities to which a banking association must necessarily be liable.

The dangers of an excessive capital, concentrated in associations invested with the attributes and privileges of a corporate body, are undeniable, and have been lately sufficiently exemplified. That danger is greatly increased, if the duration of such associations is indefinite. This had always been attended to. No bank had ever been chartered in this State with a capital exceeding two millions of dollars; and none could either increase or reduce it without the consent of the Legislature. With the exception of two institutions, incorporated for other objects, the duration of a bank did not exceed twenty-five years. No provision was made in either respect by the free banking law; and as a specimen of the expectations of the first projectors, we annex a statement of the applications made during the first six months after the law had gone into operation.

Name and Style of Company.	Where located.	Capital subscribed.	May be increased to	Chartered for
		Dollars.	Dollars.	Years.
Bank of Western New York . .	New York city	500,000	500,000	100
Bank of Western New York . .	Rochester	180,000	180,000	100
North American Trust & Banking Co.	New York city	2,000,000	50,000,000	463
Bank of the United States in New York	New York city	200,000	50,000,000	62
Mechanics' Banking Association .	New York city	128,175	10,000,000	99
Staten Island Bank . . .	PortRichmond	100,000	5,000,000	100
Erie County Bank . . .	Buffalo	100,000	100,000	112
Lockport Bank and Trust Company	Lockport	500,000	2,000,000	262
Bank of Central New York . .	Utica	100,000	2,000,000	4050
Bank of Syracuse . . .	Syracuse	100,000	1,000,000	500
American Exchange Bank . .	New York city	500,000	50,000,000	100
Farmers' Bank of Orleans . .	Gaines	200,000	500,000	25
St. Lawrence Bank ' . . .	Ogdensburgh	100,000	2,000,000	100
Merchants' and Farmers' Bank	Ithaca	150,000	2,000,000	201
Willoughby Bank . . .	Brooklyn	100,000	100,000	100
Stuyvesant Banking Company .	New York city	300,000	2,000,000	199
New-York Banking Company .	New York city	1,000,000	20,000,000	100
East River Bank of the City of New York	New York city	100,000	25,000,000	152
Chelsea Bank	New York city	1,000,000	10,000,000	150
Farmers' Bank of Ovid . .	Ovid	100,000	1,000,000	112
Tenth Ward Bank . . .	New York city	100,000	10,000,000	462
Bank of Waterville . . .	Waterville	100,000	1,000,000	1000
Millers' Bank of New York . .	Clyde	300,000	1,000,000	1000
Albany Exchange Bank. . .	Albany	100,000	10,000,000	602
Exchange Bank of Genesee .	Alexander	100,000	500,000	162
Farmers & Mechanics Bank of Genesee	Batavia	100,000	1,000,000	162
Genesee County Bank . .	Le Roy	100,000	1,000,000	161
United States Bank of Buffalo .	Buffalo	100,000	5,000,000	200
Bank of Kinderhook . . .	Kinderhook	125,000	300,000	50
Merchants' Exchange Bank of Buffalo	Buffalo	200,000	5,000,000	100
Le Roy Bank of Genesee .	Le Roy	100,000	1,000,000	161
Mechanics' and Farmers' Bank .	Ithaca	100,000	1,000,000	362
Genesee Central Bank . . .	Attica	100,000	1,000,000	300
Wool Growers' Bank of the State of NY.	New York city	100,000	2,000,000	100
Bank of Lowville . . .	Lowville	100,000	500,000	463
Erie Canal Trust & Banking Company	Buffalo	200,000	10,000,000	300
Hudson River Bank . . .	New York city	100,000	20,000,000	150
Powell Bank	Newburgh	130,000	1,000,000	100
Patriot Bank of Genesee . .	Batavia	100,000	1,000,000	161
Bank of Brockport . . .	Brockport	150,000	1,000,000	160
Ithaca Bank	Ithaca	250,000	1,000,000	662
Deposite Bank of Albany .	Albany	100,000	5,000,000	161
Bank of Waterford . .	Waterford	100,000	5,000,000	161
Silver Lake Bank of Genesee . .	Perry Village	100,000	1,000,000	161
Bank of the City of New York .	New York city	100,000	50,000,000	500
Fort Plain Bank . . .	Fort Plain	100,000	500,000	161
Troy Exchange Bank . . .	Troy	100,000	10,000,000	661
United States Trust & Banking Compy	New York city	1,000,000	50,000,000	500
Railroad Bank of Coxsackie . .	Coxsackie	100,000	1,000,000	161
James Bank	Jamesville*	106,000	1,000,000	661
North Bank	New York city	100,000	10,000,000	462
Bank of Warsaw . . .	Warsaw	100,000	1,000,000	161
Bank of North America . .	New York city	100,000	50,000,000	200
State Stock Security Bank . .	New York city			
	* Saratoga co.	12,319,175	487,680,000	

It is sufficiently apparent, from the provisions of the act, that the free banking associations, though not designated by the obnoxious name of corporations, and though organised under a general law, and not by a special charter, have all the essential and necessary attributes of a corporation. From the moment they are organised, they are in character assimilated with the chartered banks. They are, as joint stock companies, governed in the same manner, and with the same defects inherent to such companies which have already been mentioned. They have the same power and privileges, are liable to the same abuses, and differ only in name, and in that they are exempted from the restrictions imposed on the chartered banks (*rr*).

It must be kept in mind, that all the arguments in favor of banking, not simply free to all, but free also of any restriction, are founded on the presumption that the character and personal responsibility of the banker or bankers afford a sufficient security, and preferable, as is asserted, to any derived from restrictions. It is evident that, when the shareholders are not personally responsible, as was the case in every system of free banking ever attempted anywhere prior to the New York experiment, some other permanent guarantee, and not depending exclusively on the character of directors, who are not always the same, must be provided. It is on that account that precautions are necessary, not only for the payment, but also for the preservation of the capital, which is the guarantee substituted for that responsibility. This is, in fact, the object of the restrictions imposed on the chartered banks.

(*rr*) The free banking law is, at least, so generally understood. The new associations have, by the judgment of the Court for the Correction of Errors, been declared, not to be bodies politic or corporate within the spirit and meaning of the constitution. The decision thus expressed might seem to leave it doubtful whether they were not, however, monied corporations within the spirit and meaning of the Revised Statutes: in which case, they would be subject to all the general laws respecting such corporations. But it was provided by the act of 14th May 1840, that no such association should issue notes not payable on demand and without interest, and that all those associations should be subject to the inspection of the bank commissioners; which would have been unnecessary had those institutions been considered as monied corporations; since all of those having banking powers were made subject to both those provisions by the Safety Fund act.

The original free banking act did not forbid the issuing of post notes; it has in that respect been amended; but the law, as it now stands, contains no provision forbidding the dealing in stocks, nor in relation to the amount either of loans, discounts and other investments, or of the debts, which the new banking associations may contract. They are authorised to loan money on real security, and are generally, with respect to their operations, left still more free than the United States Bank of Pennsylvania. Those restrictions might, by the ardent friends of free banking, be deemed useless, if the shareholders were personally responsible; they become necessary when there is no such responsibility. There are other provisions now in force with respect to chartered banks, the propriety of which, in reference to the new associations, cannot, it is believed, be disputed.

Although the law was passed during the general suspension of the banks, no efficient provision is found in it to guard against the recurrence of the same catastrophe. The only penalty, in that respect, is the obligation to pay damages, at the rate of fourteen per cent. per year on bank notes, the payment of which is demanded and refused. And experience has proved that a similar provision was, in case of a general suspension, almost nugatory. But there is none in the act, either for constraining the associations, which shall have suspended their payments, to discontinue their operations, nor for a dissolution, as the necessary consequence of not resuming specie payments within a year. The Chancellor is authorised to dissolve the institution, only in case it shall have violated some of the provisions of the act; that is to say, in case it should not have the amount of specie required, or should have made dividends with a reduced capital, or have failed in transmitting the semi-annual statements to the Comptroller (s). But, under the law, as it now stands, there is nothing to prevent associations, which have suspended their payments, from continuing their operations during an unlimited term of years.

(s) Even those statements are complex, partly unintelligible, and differently understood and prepared by the several associations.

The only object which seems to have attracted the attention of the Legislature, is, not the danger of a suspension, but the ultimate redemption of the notes put in circulation. The provision in reference to that object is the only condition, not imposed on the chartered banks, to which the new associations are subject. They must deposit with the Comptroller certain securities, equal in amount to that of the bank notes which they are permitted to issue.

This provision, even as now amended, secures the ultimate redemption of about nine-tenths of the circulation; it is no protection against the immediate depreciation of the notes whenever the banking association fails or suspends. Those only who can wait realize that portion which is ultimately recovered by the sale of the securities. In the meanwhile, the notes dispersed in very small sums, amongst a number of persons, generally those who are least able to discriminate, are sold at a lower price than even their actual worth; and the loss falls on those least able to bear it and who require protection. It is the belief of the writer, that this provision is in fact injurious; inasmuch as it gives an unmerited credit to institutions which do not deserve it, and inspires a general unfounded confidence, on the part of those who from their situation cannot have the information necessary to discriminate between a good and a doubtful bank note (t). On one point, at least, there can be but one opinion: nominal restrictions or provisions which do not fulfil the object for which they were intended, ought to be repealed.

The consequences of the act have been nearly such as might have been expected. Several respectable associations have been formed under the law, with the intention of carrying on honestly legitimate banking business. Three such are now in operation in this city, one of which has committed the error of having part of its small capital paid in mortgages. All three carry on their business, and are governed on the same

(t) It would be extremely desirable, that the people might be persuaded to adopt as a general rule, never to receive or offer in payment a bank note not payable at the place where it is offered.

principles and in the same manner, as the chartered banks. It may be added, that they have also been formed in the same manner. A number of persons unite themselves, in order to establish a bank, take a part of the capital, invite afterwards others to unite with them, and generally preserve the control of the bank. Whether it be the chartered Bank of the State of New York, or the free Bank of Commerce, the process in the formation of both is the same. The only difference in that respect is, that the founders of the one were obliged to obtain the special leave of the Legislature, and that those of the other were enabled to make their arrangements under the auspices of a general law. There can be no doubt that, under such a law, if new, real and honest banks are wanted, they will be formed, and that, when they are found not to be profitable, there will be no desire to increase their number. Under the present imperfect system of free banking, there is, however, this difference between the two species, that the confidence placed in the new associations rests exclusively on the personal standing and character of those who control them; whilst that which is placed in the chartered banks is founded, not only on the personal character of the directors and officers, but also on the guarantee offered by the restraints imposed on them by law. Limited confidence only can be placed in joint stock companies, which are not laid under efficient restrictions, and subject to strict inspection and examination. The character of the president and directors of the Bank of the United States was as irreproachable, as that of the directors and officers of any of the banking institutions of New York.

But if some banks, formed and governed on sound principles, have been established under the free banking law, it may also give birth to associations of a different character. Some have their origin in ignorance, others in the sanguine expectations of bold speculators; occasionally they may be founded in fraud. One of the most common errors has been the belief, that an association, the capital of which consisted exclusively of mortgages, could carry on profitably ordinary banking operations. It is clear, that such an institution has nothing to lend but the notes which it may be authorised to issue, and the deposits which it may receive ; and that, whatever confidence may be placed in its ultimate means, there can be none in its available resources. The largest association of this description has hardly attempted to put its notes in circulation ; it has hardly been known as a banking institution, properly so called. But, whatever may have been the nature of its operations, and although it is hardly possible that its mortgages should be worth less than one half of their nominal value, the market price of its stock is not more than ten or twelve per cent. In this case the loss, so far as is known, falls only on the shareholders. But the conclusive proof of the unsoundness of the system is found in the fact that, out of about eighty associations, formed under the law, more than twenty have failed in the course of two years and a half (u) ; whilst, as has already been stated, two only, out of the ninety chartered banks, have failed during a period of ten years.

The numerous failures of country bankers in England, in particular years, have already been alluded to. A more correct view of the subject will be obtained by taking the average of a number of years. The number of commissions of bankruptcy issued, during the twelve years, 1814 to 1825, against bankers, amounted to one hundred and ninety-four; the number of bankers was estimated to amount to about one thousand. The ratio of failures to the number of bankers was, therefore, sixteen per cent. in ten years. The ratio of failures to the number of chartered banks, in the State of New York, has been less than two and a quarter per cent. during the last ten years. Here, we compare personally responsible private bankers with banks, in which the capital actually paid has been the guarantee substituted for personal responsibility, and which have been regulated by efficient restrictions. The assertions, that the community will be better protected, and individuals of all classes less likely to be imposed upon, under a system in which there is neither personal responsibility, nor any assurance of a sufficient and real capital actually paid, nor any legal restrictions that

---

(u) The securities of twelve of these, which had been deposited with the Comptroller, are at this moment advertised for sale by him, in order to pay their circulation.

may prevent the dilapidation of that capital, is a pure theoretical opinion wholly unsustained by experience.

Whenever an application is made, either for the reduction of the capital of a chartered bank, or for the renewal of the charter, or even for changing the location of a bank from one street to another, these banks continue to be represented as privileged bodies; and they are invited to surrender their charters, and to convert themselves into free associations' under the general law.

It is extraordinary that intelligent men should still consider the chartered banks as enjoying exclusive privileges. The monopoly is now destroyed; and all persons, or associations of persons, may now establish banks on more easy terms than those imposed on the chartered institutions, and with all the privileges enjoyed by them. If any importance be attached to the obligation of depositing an amount of State stocks or mortgages, equal to that circulation, though useless and even injurious, it may easily be extended by a legislative act to the chartered banks. But, if the enemies of monopolies will only take the trouble to examine the general laws respecting monied corporations and the special charters of the banks, they will find that these banks do not enjoy a single privilege which is not common to the free banking associations; and that what they are pleased to call privileges, consists, on the contrary, altogether of restrictions. There is not now the slightest foundation for the assertion, and it has become quite senseless.

Two things are requisite, in order that the chartered banks may convert themselves into free associations; first, that a law should be enacted for that purpose; secondly, that the free banking law should be so modified as to make the conversion proper.

There is not now any oth r legal mode, by which the conversion can be effected, than by a dissolution of the corporation, and a subsequent association of the shareholders. The manner in which a corporation can be voluntarily dissolved, is prescribed by law. The process would last one or two years, during which the bank must suspend all its active operations; and, in order to accomplish the object, it must pay all its liabilities before the shareholders can have access to the capital, and either divide it, or form with it a new association. It must therefore, in the first instance, lose all its deposits and redeem all its circulation, and then, at the end of two years, begin anew without either. Every person practically acquainted with banking, knows that, under this process, five or six years would elapse before the bank could recover its former situation.

But, even if a law were passed authorising the immediate transmutation, no sound·bank would, or at least ought to, avail itself of the provision; for if it did, it would immediately lose the public confidence. It would at once be presumed, that a bank pursuing that course wanted to be free of restrictions, to launch into some speculative operation, and to escape responsibility. The fact is, that the greater confidence, placed in the chartered banks, is entirely due to the restrictions imposed by law upon them.

It is at the same time highly desirable, that all the banks and banking associations should be placed under the same regimen, and by virtue of a general law, instead of special charters or any special legislation. It seems that this might have been done with great facility, at the time when the free banking law was enacted. Nothing more was necessary, in order to destroy the monopoly, than a short act authorising the forming of free associations, with all the corporate attributes given by the present law, but precisely on the same terms, which are imposed on the chartered banks by the general laws of the State. This would at once have placed all on an equal footing. This having been done, an examination of those laws and the lessons of experience would have enabled the Legislature to select and modify such of the existing restrictions, and to add such new conditions, as in its opinion were proper and necessary. Whether the system, thus adopted, had embraced few or many restrictions, or had repealed them altogether, that which was proper and necessary for the new associations was equally so for all the chartered banks carrying on the same business. The power reserved by the Legislature, to modify and alter any charter, extended to all the chartered banks, with the single exception of the Manhattan, and perhaps of the Dry Dock Company. The four other banks, not under the Safety Fund, are understood to have assented, in conformily with the Suspension Act, that the Legislature might modify or repeal their charters.

There does not seem to be, at present, any serious obstacle to the same course of proceeding. No special act, affecting singly any one of the new banking associations, can be passed; but the Legislature may at any time *alter* or repeal the act itself. Vested interests must be respected; and for that purpose, it would be sufficient to limit the duration of all such existing associations to a limited term of years, and their capital to the amount actually paid at the time when the new amended law did pass. The restrictions, deemed necessary and proper by the Legislature, would then be extended to all the existing free associations and chartered banks, as well as to all other free associations which might thereafter be formed. The object should be, that all the charters should merge in the general law; and that the law should be precisely the same for all those engaged in the same pursuit. What restrictions should, in the opinion of the writer, be preserved or added, have already been fully stated.

It is believed, and the belief is corroborated by the result of private banking in England, and by what is known respecting the new joint stock companies of that country, that there is danger in granting the unrestricted power of issuing a paper currency, even when accompanied by the personal responsibility of those who issue the paper. But this applies only to notes of a certain denomination. Notes of one hundred dollars, and of a higher denomination, circulate almost exclusively between dealers and dealers, and might, like bills of exchange, be permitted to circulate without any restrictions, or other guarantee than the personal responsibility of the persons or associations by whom they were issued.

ACTION OF CONGRESS.

The objects to which, in reference to currency, the powers vested in the General Government may, it is believed, be applied, and which will probably become, at this time, subjects of discussion, are the Sub-Treasury, a Bank of the United States, and a Bankrupt Law.

The Government of the United States has the undoubted right to entrust the custody of the public monies to its own officers; and this is sometimes necessary. It may also, and every individual has the same right for debts due to him, require the payment of taxes, and other branches of the revenue, to be made exclusively in gold or silver. And it is bound to carry into effect the provision of the constitution, which directs that all duties, imposts and excises shall be uniform throughout the United States.

From the time when the Government was organised, till very lately, it had been thought safer, whenever it was practicable, to commit the custody of the public monies to banks, rather than to intrust them to the officers of Government; and there is no doubt in that respect, whenever the money can be deposited in sound and specie-paying banks. In that opinion the whole community coincides. The character of the late, as well as that of the present receiver for the city of New York, is irreproachable. Yet it would be difficult to find any individual in his senses, who would not deposit his money in a sound city bank, rather than in the hands of the receiver. The capital of the bank is a better security than the bonds of any private person; and the banks are answerable for contingent losses, such as fire or robbery, for which a public officer cannot be made responsible. So long, also, as the bank currency remains equivalent to the precious metals, it is much more convenient both for Government, for those who have duties to pay, and for all the parties concerned. to conform to the general usage rather than to require payments in specie.

But the depreciated currency of banks, which have suspended

specie payments, cannot be received in payment of duties and of other taxes, without a violation of the principles of justice, and of the positive injunction of the constitution. And instances may occur in some sections of the country, where it would be unsafe even to make a special deposit of the public monies in any bank in that section. At a time when one half of the public revenue is collected in places where all the banks have suspended specie payments, Treasury notes appear to afford the most convenient means of complying with the constitution, and of rendering the duties uniform throughout the United States (v). Some other means of accomplishing that object must be devised, if it should please Congress to suppress the use of those notes, and to repeal altogether the Sub-Treasury act.

The specie clause, as it is called, of the act is, however, liable to serious objections. It had already been previously provided, that the Secretary of the Treasury should not employ any bank which had suspended specie payments. The new provision, which extended the prohibition to all the banks without exception, was in fact operative against those banks alone which continued to pay in specie. Those who had duties to pay might be annoyed; but it was quite immaterial to the banks which had ceased to pay any of their liabilities in specie, whether the duties were paid in coin; the demand for it did not fall upon them. It was quite otherwise in the places where specie payments were sustained; and the law in that respect, though probably not thus intended, was a warfare directed exclusively against those institutions which performed their duty, and, not without some difficulty, sustained a sound currency. It is true that, in the actual state of things, and whilst the revenue falls short of the expenses, the law, though occasionally annoying, does not produce any sensible effect; but this also proves that it was not necessary.

Whenever the revenue shall exceed the expenditure, the law

(v) The Treasury notes are a mere transcript of the English Exchequer bills. Used as soberly as they have been of late years by the Treasury Department, and provided they are kept at par, they are the most convenient mode of supplying a temporary deficiency in the revenue; as well as the most convenient substitute for currency, in the payment of duties, during a suspension of specie payments.

will operate, and, if the excess should again be considerable, the drain of specie this would occasion, might indeed break any bank, and render the suspension of specie payments universal. It cannot be perceived, in what manner the measure can, in any way whatever, have a tendency towards restoring a general sound currency. It is utterly impossible to substitute, otherwise than very gradually, a currency consisting exclusively of the precious metals, for that which now pervades the whole country.

Any great accumulation of the public monies is attended with such evils, that it must at all events be averted. If consisting of gold and silver accumulated in the Treasury chest, it is an active capital taken from the people and rendered unproductive. If deposited in banks, or consisting of bank paper, it may again produce a fatal expansion of the discounts and issues of the banks, attended by over-trading, and followed by contractions and a general derangement.

Another objection to the law was that, with the exception of Congress and of the officers of the General Government, it seemed as if the whole community was opposed to the measure. If necessary and proper for that Government, it was equally so for that of every individual State. And yet it was not adopted, or even proposed, by the Legislature of a single State. On the contrary, even in some of those most friendly, and to the last most faithful, to the late Administration, a direct and legal sanction was given to the collection of the State revenue in a depreciated and irredeemable currency, instead of requiring payment in specie, as was done by the act of Congress.

This country had a sound currency, and there was no general suspension of specie payments, so long as either of the two Banks of the United States was in existence. The refusal to renew the charters was, in both instances, followed by a large increase of State banks, and shortly after by a general suspension of payments. The resumption which took place in 1817, immediately followed, and has been generally ascribed to, the establishment of the second national bank. Notwithstanding the efforts of the banks of New York and of New England, subsequent to the suspension of 1837, a general resumption has not yet taken place. A considerable portion of the commercial community therefore hopes, that a new Bank of the United States will accelerate such resumption, and again secure a currency equivalent to gold and silver. This confidence, if sustained by a proper administration of the contemplated bank, might go far towards attaining the object in view. Confidence is certainly a most powerful element in sustaining any system of paper currency.

On the other hand, a national bank has ever been, and, from its nature, must be, generally unpopular. It will always be assailed by those who are opposed generally to banks; by many, as not warranted by the constitution; and at present, from considerations connected with the state of parties. It must also be admitted that great power is always liable to be abused; and it cannot be doubted, that the catastrophe of the United States Bank has shaken confidence, and given additional strength to the arguments against a bank of that name and character, and with such a large capital.

These considerations render it necessary to act with great caution and due deliberation; to form a just estimate of the advantages which may be expected from the intended bank; and to inquire by what provisions the substantial objections against the institution may be obviated.

The opinions of the writer respecting the constitutional powers of Congress, the great utility of a national bank as the fiscal agent of Government, and the aid which may be derived from it to regulate the general currency of the country, are the same as heretofore. The constitutional question has been so long and in so many shapes under consideration, that the subject appears to be exhausted; and nothing needs be added in that respect. Independently of the temporary accommodations which a Bank of the United States affords to Government, when required to supply a temporary deficiency in the revenue, and of the advances which it may, in extraordinary times, make to the contractors of public loans, there cannot be any doubt that, as regards the security and transmission of public monies and the general convenience of the Treasury, a national bank is far preferable to those of individual States. The experience of the writer, under both systems, permits him to make the assertion with perfect confidence.

The only way in which a Bank of the United States can regulate the local currencies, is by keeping its own loans and discounts within narrow bounds, and rigorously requiring a regular payment of the balances due to it by the State banks. The object might be attained without its aid, in places where the local banks will, by adopting the same course, check each other and regulate themselves. Where this does not take place, the interference of the National Bank is of great importance and highly useful. But the measure is practically difficult and generally unpopular; though it might be rendered more palatable, if the bank was forbidden to use the public deposits, beyond a certain amount, for its own benefit.

This favorable result may be reasonably expected whenever a general resumption shall have taken place. But doubts may be entertained, whether, under existing circumstances, the bank can cause a general resumption without the aid of State legislation, or the co-operation of the State banks; and it is perfectly clear, that it cannot act as a regulator of local currencies, in those places where the banks, from any cause whatever, continue to suspend their specie payments. It would seem necessary to ascertain in what places, and particularly in which of the great centres of commerce, a National Bank is desired, and, from the confidence it might inspire, would induce a resumption.

Some other advantages, of a more doubtful nature, seem to be expected from a Bank of the United States; such as an increase of commercial facilities; a greater uniformity in domestic exchanges; and a hope that its notes may, to a great extent, advantageously supersede those of the local banks.

An increase of the mass of commercial loans is not at all desirable. The number of banks and the amount of their discounts is already too great; and in order to be useful, the effect of the loans and of the circulation of the National Bank, should be to lessen, and not to increase, the gross amount of both.

The great inequality and fluctuations of the domestic exchanges, so far as they are the result of depreciated currencies, cannot be remedied by a Bank of the United States, as long as they continue to be the local circulating medium. After that evil shall have been removed by a resumption of specie payments, the bank cannot and ought not to interfere, any farther than as purchasers and sellers of exchange and drafts, in the same manner as other money dealers. It is only as an additional dealer, with greater funds and facilities than any other, that the bank may bring exchange nearer to par, or, in other words, transmit on cheaper terms funds from one place to another, as they may be wanted.

But it is a great error to suppose that it can afford a generally uniform currency; or one which shall, at the same time, be of the same value in all places. This is to confound exchange and currency, and to suppose that paper money may not only be a true representative of gold and silver, but can perform that which gold and silver cannot accomplish.

The fluctuations in the rate of exchange, like those in the market price of commodities, depend on the relative amount of supply and demand; and these again on the relative indebtedness and the actual means of making remittances. When American coins can purchase in New York bills on London, which will produce there an amount of British coins, containing as much pure gold as was contained in the American coins with which the bills were purchased, it is called the true par of exchange. If the amount of British coins, obtained in London for the bills, contain less pure gold than the American coins paid for the bills, it is a clear proof, that the same quantity of pure gold is worth less in New York than in London; and this cannot be altered by substituting in New York, for coin, a paper money which has no other property than that of being convertible into coin at New York at its nominal value. The case is precisely the same between New Orleans and New York, or between any two places whatever.

A National Bank may find it possible, and convenient, to give occasional facilities in that respect. But it can no more issue a currency necessarily payable, at the option of the holder, in several places, than a merchant can bind himself to be ready to pay a debt at five or six different places, at the option of his creditor and without notice.

If the bank should issue all its notes payable at one place, they would be currency at the place of issue; and, in every other place, they would be worth more or less than the local currency, or than gold or silver, according to the rate of exchange between such places respectively, and the place of issue where alone they were made payable. If the notes are, as heretofore, made payable at various places, such issues will make part of the local currency of the places where they are respectively made payable, and cannot pay debts elsewhere, any more than the notes of local banks.

It would seem generally to follow, that the circulation of a Bank of the United States cannot be otherwise extended, than in as far as it may supersede the local currencies of the several States. In former times, that circulation was principally in the South and in the West, as will appear by the following authentic statement of the places where the notes in actual circulation of the Bank of the United States were payable, in September, 1830 :—

Payable in New England	$834,492
" New York	834,733
" Philadelphia	1,367,180
" Baltimore and Washington	1,176,240
" the Southern States	3,074,045
" the N. Western States, including Buffalo and Pittsburg	3,261,547
" the South-Western States	4,799,420
	$15,347,657

It may be doubted whether a similar proportionate amount can now be circulated in quarters which have become saturated with paper money. It is not impossible that this may take place in those States where the evils of a depreciated currency have become intolerable.

An additional demand, to a moderate amount, for notes, principally of five dollars, payable at New York or Philadelphia, may also be expected on account of their great convenience in travelling, and for small remittances. Checks and bills of exchange are safer and more convenient than bank notes, for large remittances.

If a Bank of the United States can, notwithstanding the obstacles of conflicting opinions and interests, be again created by Congress, it will be necessary to guard against the evils which such an institution may produce. The views of the writer, such as they are, have already been stated in the preceding pages. Those provisions that seem most important, in reference to a National Bank, will be recapitulated.

The danger of an abuse of the power, which must necessarily be given, is increased in proportion to the magnitude of the capital. This should not be greater than is necessary for the object intended. The bank is not wanted in order to increase the amount of commercial accommodations. A small capital would suffice for its operations, in its character of fiscal agent of the Government. For the purpose of regulating, as far as practicable, the local currencies, it is not necessary that, at least at first, it should be extended beyond the great centres of commerce. The power hereafter, if found requisite, to increase the capital, might be reserved by Congress. A large capital is not wanted for the purpose of sustaining an adequate circulation; and this may be increased, without danger, beyond its ordinary limits, provided the amounts of loans and discounts be kept within narrow bounds. The Bank of England, with a capital of fourteen millions sterling, sustains a circulation of at least eighteen millions. The Bank of France, with a capital of sixty-eight millions of francs, (about thirteen millions of dollars,) has a circulation of two hundred and forty millions, and generally in its vaults two hundred and thirty millions of specie. It may be added, that, under existing circumstances, the plan may fail altogether, unless the amount required be moderate (w).

It is believed that a capital of fifteen millions of dollars, paid altogether in specie, or in bank notes equivalent to specie, would be amply sufficient. To this may be added, if deemed eligible, and to be viewed as an ultimate guarantee, five millions of dollars in a five per cent. stock of the United States. The bank should not be authorised to dispose of that stock, without the leave of Congress, or perhaps of the Treasury Department. No other description of stocks should be admitted as part of the capital.

Besides the restrictions imposed by the charter of the late

(w) The views of the writer have in that respect been modified since the year 1811, by observations abroad, by practical banking experience at home, and by the aberrations of the late Bank of the United States.

bank, the amount of loans, discounts, and all other investments bearing an interest, should be limited, so as not to exceed once and a half the amount of the capital, or, at most, sixty per cent. beyond it. It has already been shown, that, with that limitation, after the maximum of such investments has been reached, the amount of specie must necessarily increase with that of circulation and deposits. When such reciprocal increase takes place naturally, it produces no inconvenience. If it should be the result of a considerable increase of accumulated revenue, it will produce the same evils which, under any circumstances, are the consequence of such an increase. Taxes to a large amount would be intolerable, if they were not expended, and if the money drawn from the people was not immediately restored to circulation. But if, notwithstanding the measures which may be adopted by Government, in order to prevent an undue accumulation, this should occasionally take place, the restriction on the amount of loans and discounts will prevent the application to that object of the excess of public deposits. Whether the amount of specie in the bank should be increased from that cause, or by a natural extension of its circulation and individual deposits, that specie will afford an ample security for the payment of all the liabilities of the institution. In that case, the bank would be the great reservoir which might, if applied properly, supply sudden demands, and, at critical times, sustain the other banks, protect the local currency, and lessen the commercial distress.

It is presumed that the ordinary restrictions, forbidding to deal in real estate, merchandise or stocks, will be retained, and that the bank will be confined strictly to pure and legitimate banking operations.

The provisions which have been already suggested in case of a suspension of specie payments, appear indispensable, as well as one which will declare the bank to be necessarily dissolved, if the suspension continues more than a year.

Whether the bank should absolutely be forbidden to issue post notes; and whether a limitation on the amount of dividends, which in fact will be limited by the restrictions on the amount of loans and discounts, be necessary; are questions which may deserve consideration. But, in order to enforce the restrictions and conditions of the charter, whatever they may be, a rigorous and regular inspection by officers appointed by Government is absolutely necessary. The power to make occasional examinations by committees of either branch of the Legislature may be reserved, but is not adequate to the purpose. In that respect, the law of New York, for the establishment of bank commissioners, may serve as a model. It has been tested by the experience of ten years, and has been attended with none but beneficial results. The power given to them, to inspect all the books and papers, without excepting the accounts of individuals, and that of examining upon oath all the officers of every bank, and every other person, concerning its affairs, are both necessary and have never been abused. In the case under consideration, the commissioners would naturally be placed under the superintendence of the Treasury Department. The appointment of directors by Government may be useful, but is less important.

Amongst many suggestions that have been made, and which deserve consideration, there is one which appears important, principally in order that the bank may have a truly national character and not degenerate into a local institution. It is proposed that the general control of the bank should be separated from the local business of the place where it may be located. Nothing more is meant by this, than that the office of discount and deposit for that place should be as distinct from the general direction, as the branches which are located in other places ; and that such office should be considered simply as one of the branches. In that case, the members of the general direction might be but few; no more than one or two from any one State ; and it would, therefore, be necessary, in order to secure the constant attendance of those from other States than that in which the main bank was located, that they should receive a competent and even liberal salary. But this general board, though separated from the office of discount, must still necessarily sit in a great commercial city.

The constitution of the United States provides, that Congress shall have power to establish an uniform rule of naturalisation, and uniform laws on the subject of bankruptcies throughout the United States.

The true meaning of the word "bankruptcies" has been questioned. But whether, according to the sense in which the word was generally used and understood at the time when the constitution was adopted, it embraces all persons unable or unwilling to pay their debts, or is confined only to traders and dealers, it is conceded on all hands, that it is applicable to all who are universally admitted to be traders or dealers. And it cannot be denied that bankers, or dealers in money, are included within that description.

In other respects the power is given in express terms, and in the most general manner. It is, to pass laws *on the subject* of bankruptcies. Congress is not, therefore, bound by the specific provisions of the pre-existing laws, on that subject, of any country. It may define what acts shall constitute bankruptcy; what shall be the remedy in reference both to the creditor and to the debtor; and what shall be the mode of proceeding. The question to be examined is, whether the law shall apply to banking corporations. The intrinsic propriety of including those institutions can hardly be denied; and no act of Congress could be more useful and efficient, for the purpose of securing a general sound currency.

The general evil under which the whole country labors, is that, owing to the dissimilar, imperfect, fluctuating, or relaxed legislation of the several States, those institutions or corporate bodies which have been permitted to issue a paper currency, on the express condition that it should be at all times redeemable, on demand, in gold or silver, are suffered with impunity to break their engagements, and to pay their debts in a depreciated paper, not equivalent to that which, by the constitution, is declared to be the only tender in payment of debts. A law which shall declare it to be an act of bankruptcy, on the part of all those who issue notes or evidences of debt to be put in circulation as money (y), to continue, for a certain length of time, to decline or refuse to redeem in specie such notes or bills, would afford the most general and efficient preventive and remedy

---

(y) These are the technical words used in the law of New York, in relation to the issuing and circulation of bank notes.

that can be devised. It would alone be sufficient to arrest the evil, to place all the States on a footing of equality, and to restore and maintain the soundness of all the local currencies.

The laws of the same purport, enacted by New York, and by some other States, are in fact bankrupt laws applied to that special object. Those States, and all those which maintain, or are desirous of maintaining specie payments and a sound currency, are deeply interested in making the law general. It must also be observed, that incorporated banks enjoy already all the privileges which a bankrupt law can afford to debtors; that is to say, that, on surrendering all the property which belongs to the corporation, no further demand can be made either against it, nor, in their individual capacity, against its members. It is, therefore, strictly consistent with justice, that they should be made subject to the provisions of that branch of the bankrupt law, which is intended to protect the creditors. In point of fact, the whole, or almost the whole, banking business of the United States is carried on by incorporated banks. To exempt them from the operation of a general law is, not only the grant of a banking monopoly, but an exclusive privilege in favor of a special class of dealers; and the occupation of those dealers, that of substituting a paper for a specie currency, is of all others the most dangerous to the community, and that which requires to be most strictly restrained by legal enactments, instead of being exempt from the provisions of a law, which applies to every other description of dealers.

Although the great utility and strict justice of the application, of a general bankrupt law to incorporated banks may not be denied; it seems that the power of Congress in that respect has been questioned, by some persons, as an infringement of the rights of the States, and as not being warranted by the constitution. The object of this essay is to suggest such provisions as appear useful and practicable, on subjects which are familiar to the writer, rather than to discuss constitutional questions, which may be beyond his competency. But, in this instance, the objection seems so extraordinary, that some desultory observations may be permitted.

The power to establish uniform laws on the subject of bankruptcies throughout the United States, is not implied but express; and it is given in the most general and extensive terms that could be devised, without any other limitation than that which may be deduced from the meaning of the word "bankruptcies," and which does not apply to the question under consideration. The laws must be uniform. It may perhaps be said, that the condition of uniformity is not violated, by exempting from the operation of the law a certain class of dealers, provided all the dealers of that description are exempted. But this would be a dangerous principle. The power of passing laws on the subject of bankruptcies, like that to regulate commerce among the several States, of which it is in fact only a part, must be uniform in every respect. To permit every other species of property to be freely carried from one State to another, and to except slaves, by forbidding their being transported from one slaveholding to another slaveholding State, would certainly be considered as a direct violation of the constitution.

The power of the several States, to create corporations or artificial bodies is universally acknowledged. And, although the privilege may not be absolutely essential, yet as by usage it is almost universal, the power to confine the responsibility to the property owned by the corporation as such, and to make its members irresponsible, is also admitted. But it is not perceived, on what principle, those artificial bodies can in any other respect be, any more than natural persons, rightfully exempted from the legitimate general laws of the United States. Such exemption has not heretofore been claimed. The incorporated banks may, in many instances, be sued in the courts of the United States. Judgments may be obtained in those courts against them, and execution levied on their corporate property. Their real estate is liable to taxation, whenever the United States lay a direct tax on property of that description. Their notes were made liable to the stamp duty, in common with the notes of private individuals. The individual States might have claimed the right to exempt those institutions in all those respects, with as much propriety, as in reference to a bankrupt law. The claim might be extended to all other associations of persons, incorporated for establishing manufactures, or for any other enterprise whatever; and associations, not only for carrying on manufactories, but also fisheries, the fur trade, and other species of business, have actually been incorporated by some of the States.

A system of free banking has been introduced into the State of New York, by authorising associations for that purpose, which are not by law considered as corporations; and it is hoped that the system will become general and operate a conversion of all the chartered banks into free and not incorporated associations. Would it be just that they should be subject to the bankrupt law, whilst the chartered banks remained exempted from its operation?

It may perhaps be alleged that, inasmuch as the States have respectively passed laws ,providing for the manner in which the property of the incorporated banks may be sequestered, placed in the hands of trustees or receivers, and be distributed amongst the creditors, the United States have no right to interfere, and to provide other means for the same purpose. But it has been generally admitted, and the doctrine is sound and rational, that so long as Congress does not exercise a discretionary power given to it by the constitution, the laws of the States on such subjects are legitimate and obligatory; but that they are superseded by the laws of Congress, whenever that body thinks it proper to exercise such discretionary power. This has happened very lately in the provisions respecting pilots: the sanction of Congress has been given to the quarantine laws of the several States: it has been adjudged, that they had the right to naturalize aliens, until Congress had passed a general law on that subject, and that, from that time, the right ceased.

Some difficulties may be suggested respecting the practicability of applying the provisions of a bankrupt law to corporations; but it is believed that they may be easily surmounted.

There are some acts, considered by the English laws as acts of bankruptcy, which could not be done by a corporation. The only consequence would be that, since the act could not be done, the law in that respect could not be applied to the incorporated banks. But Congress is not at all bound by the special provisions of the English bankrupt laws. It is generally authorised to pass laws on the subject of bankruptcies; and it may therefore define what shall be considered as acts of bankruptcy, and adapt the definition to the object in view. It has already been suggested that nothing more was wanted in reference to banks, than to make it an act of bankruptcy for all those who issue paper money, to refuse for a certain length of time to redeem it in specie.

There are also some penalties, which are inapplicable to corporations, and from which they would of course be exempted. But there is a point which deserves consideration. No bankrupt law would be passed in this age, and in this country, which would condemn a bankrupt to death. By parity of reasoning, it may be insisted that the act of Congress, which will not inflict the pain of death on the natural person, ought not to kill, or, in other words, to dissolve the artificial body. This may be granted: the power of dissolving may be left to the State which created. The essential object of a bankrupt law, with respect to the creditor, is to preserve from dilapidation the property in the possession of his debtor, and to make an equal division of it amongst all the creditors. This may be attained, without putting to death the person, or dissolving the corporate body (z).

(z) The establishment of a Mint in New York would have a tendency to sustain the currency. Foreign coins are generally exported in preference to those of the United States. A very considerable proportion of the foreign gold and silver coins, which pass through the banks of the city of New York, would be converted into American coins, if it could be done without the expense, risk, delay, and inconvenience of sending them to Philadelphia. The practical injury is much greater than may be generally supposed. It must not be forgotten that New York is the principal place of importation, and still more so of the exportation, of the precious metals; and that it is also, as being the most exposed, that which it is most important to protect against the danger of a suspension of specie payments.

APPENDIX.

DOCUMENTS RESPECTING THE RESUMPTION OF SPECIE PAYMENTS IN THE YEAR 1838.

CIRCULAR.—*To the principal Banks in the United States.*

New York, August 18th, 1837.

Sir,—At a general meeting of the officers of the banks of the city of New-York, held on the 15th of this month, the following resolution was unanimously adopted, viz:

Resolved, That a committee be appointed to correspond with such banks in the several States as they may think proper, in order to ascertain at what time and place a Convention of the principal banks should be held, for the purpose of agreeing on the time when specie payments should be resumed, and on the measures necessary to effect that purpose.

Having been appointed a committee in conformity with that resolution, we beg leave to call your attention to the important subject to which it refers.

The suspension of specie payments was forced upon the banks immediately by a panic and by causes not under their control, remotely by the unfortunate coincidence of extraordinary events and incidents, the ultimate result of which was anticipated neither by Government or by any part of the community.

But it is nevertheless undeniable, that, by accepting their charters, the banks had contracted the obligation of redeeming their issues at all times and under any circumstances whatever; that they have not been able to perform that engagement; and that a depreciated paper, differing in value in different places, and subject to daily fluctuations in the same place, has thus been substituted for the currency, equivalent to gold or silver, which, and no other, they were authorised and had the exclusive right to issue.

Such a state of things cannot, and ought not, to be tolerated any longer than an absolute necessity requires it. We are very certain that you unite with us in the opinion, that it is the paramount and most sacred duty of the banks to exert every effort, to adopt every measure within their power, which may promote and accelerate the desired result; and that they must be prepared to resume specie payments within the shortest possible notice, whenever a favorable alteration shall occur in the rate of foreign exchanges.

We are quite aware of the difficulties which must be surmounted, and of the impropriety of any premature attempt. No banking system could indeed be tolerated which was not able to withstand the ordinary and unavoidable fluctuations of exchange. But the difference is great between continuing and resuming specie payments: and we do not believe, that the banks in the United States can, without running the imminent danger of another speedy and fatal catastrophe, resume such payments before the foreign debt shall have been so far lessened or adjusted, as to reduce the rate of exchanges to true specie par, and the risk of an immediate exportation of the precious metals shall have thus been removed.

The appearances in that respect have become more flattering; and it is not improbable that the expected change may take place shortly after the next crop of our principal article of exports shall begin to operate. Yet we are sensible that we must not rely on conjectures, and that the banks cannot designate the time when they may resume, before the ability to sustain specie payments shall have been ascertained by the actual reduction in the rate of the exchanges.

But even when the apprehension of a foreign drain of specie shall have ceased, the great object in view cannot be effected without a concert of the banks in the several sections of the Union. Those of this city had the misfortune to be, with few exceptions, the first that were compelled to declare their inability to sustain, for the time, specie payments. It appears that it became absolutely necessary for the other banks to pursue the same course; and it would be likewise impracticable for those of any particular section to resume without a general co-operation of at least the principal banks of the greater part of the country. A mutual and free communication of their respective situations, prospects and opinions, seems to be a necessary preliminary step, to be followed by a Convention at such time and place as may be agreed upon.

As relates to the banks of this city, we are of opinion that, provided the co-operation of the other banks is obtained, they may, and ought to, we should perhaps say that they must, resume specie payments before next spring, or, to be more precise, between the first of January and the middle of March 1838.

Both the time and place of meeting in Convention must of course be determined in conformity with the general wishes of the banks. In order to bring the subject in a definite shape before you, we merely suggest the latter end of October as the proper time, and this city as the most eligible place for the proposed Convention.

A sufficient time will have then elapsed to enable us to judge of the measures which Congress may adopt in reference to the subject. Whatever may be its action on the currency, the duty of resuming remains the same, and must be performed by the banks. If any thing indeed can produce an effect favorable to their views, it will be the knowledge of their being sincerely and earnestly engaged in effecting that purpose. An early indication of the determination of the banks will have a beneficial influence, by making them all aware of the necessity of adopting the requisite preliminary measures; and the information is also due to all the varied interests of the country.

We address this letter to no other bank in your city or State than those herein designated; and we pray you to collect and ascertain the opinions of the others, and to communicate the general result as early as practicable.

We have the honor to be, &c.

ALBERT GALLATIN,
GEORGE NEWBOLD,
C. W. LAWRENCE,
Committee.

———

Extract from the Minutes of the Board of Delegates of the Banks of the City and Incorporated Districts of the County of Philadelphia.

At a special meeting of the delegates of all the banks in the city and the incorporated districts of the county of Philadelphia, held on Tuesday evening, August 29th, 1837, the following preamble and resolutions were, on motion, unanimously adopted, viz:

Whereas a proposition has been submitted to this meeting, on behalf of the officers of the banks of the city of New York, for calling a convention of delegates from the principal banks in the United States, to be held in New York in the month of October next, for the purpose of adopting measures for the resumption of payments in specie by the banks: after mature reflection upon this proposal, and the reasons assigned for it, this meeting has not been able to adopt the views presented in the communication; and they deem it proper to state briefly and without reserve the reasons of their dissent.

The banks of Philadelphia fully concur with the banks of New York in their anxiety for a general resumption of specie payments with the least practicable delay, and they would cordially unite in the proposed convention if they thought it at all adapted to promote that object. But they believe that the general resumption of specie payments depends mainly, if not exclusively, on the action of Congress—the body charged with the general power over commerce, and the exclusive power over the coinage, and without whose co-operation, all attempts at a general system of payments in coin throughout this extensive country must be partial and temporary.

That body is on the point of assembling, being expressly convened to deliberate on this very subject.

Now, the banks of Philadelphia are of opinion, that, at such a moment, a convention of the banks of the United States would be superfluous at least, if not injurious. It seems superfluous, because the banks can do nothing, and ought to promise nothing, until they know what the action of Congress will be. The communication from New York mentions a precise period when the banks of New York may, and ought to, and must, resume specie payments. With every respectful deference to the better judgment of the signers of the communication, the banks of Philadelphia are not prepared to make any pledges, nor to name any time, for the resumption, because they think that the whole matter depends much more on Congress than on themselves. They do not wish to excite expectations which they may not be able to realize; and they believe that a premature effort might be followed by a relapse, which would be permanently fatal to the credit of our banking institutions. If, moreover, such a convention, composed of delegates from sections of the country of very unequal resources, and in very different stages of preparation, should not agree upon any general system of action, these very discussions would weaken confidence in the convention; while, if they could agree, their union upon any course of measures might not recommend that course to public favor, because it would be considered as one specially favorable to the interests of banks themselves. It is thus that the convention might prove not merely useless, but injurious. The mere assemblage of a body, more numerous probably than Congress itself, meeting at the same time, deliberating on the same subject, might easily be made to wear the appearance of an attempt to interfere with, or to influence the movements of, that body. The avowed object of the convention too—to fix a time for resuming specie payments independent of Congress—might have the effect of misleading both Congress and the country. If the resumption be practicable by the banks alone, Congress might consider itself under no obligation to interpose—a very erroneous and dangerous conclusion. If the banks confidently name a day when they not only may, but must resume, whatever be the action of Congress, or the state of the country, or the condition of the foreign exchanges, they promise what they may not be able to perform, and so lose, rather than gain credit by the effort. A more prudent course, in the deliberate judgment of this meeting, would be for the banks in the United States to continue steadily their present preparations for resuming specie payments; to wait quietly the action of Congress, without interference of any kind; and be ready to give an immediate and zealous co-operation in any measures which that body may adopt for the common benefit of the country. Under these impressions, they are constrained to adopt the following resolutions:

Resolved, That, in the opinion of the banks of Philadelphia, it is inexpedient, at this time, to appoint delegates to the proposed convention.

Resolved, That a copy of these resolutions, certified by the President and Secretary of this meeting, be forwarded to the banks of New York, with an assurance, that while the banks of Philadelphia reluctantly differ from those of New York as to the specific measure proposed, they do ample justice to the zeal and patriotism which have dictated it; that they are not the less anxious to accomplish the common object; and that, if the proposed convention should suggest any thing which promises to be useful to the country, the banks of Philadelphia will as cordially co-operate in executing it as if they had been fully represented in the convention.

Extract from the Minutes:

W. MEREDITH, *President.*

J. B. TREVOR, *Secretary.*

———

CIRCULAR.—*To the principal Banks in the United States.*

New York, Oct. 20th, 1837.

Sir,—At a general meeting of the officers of the banks of the city of New York, held on the 10th of this month, the committee appointed on the 15th of August last, laid before the meeting the communications received from banks in the several States, in answer to the circular of the committee of the 18th of August last.

Whereupon, it was unanimously "*Resolved*, That the banks in the several States be respectfully invited to appoint delegates to meet on the 27th day of November next, in the city of New York, for the purpose of conferring on the time when specie payments may be resumed with safety, and on the measures necessary to effect that purpose."

We pray you to communicate this letter to such other banks in your State as you may deem proper; and leaving the number of delegates entirely to yourselves, we only beg leave to urge the importance of having every State represented.

We have the honor to be respectfully your most obedient servants,

ALBERT GALLATIN,
GEORGE NEWBOLD,
C. W. LAWRENCE,
Committee.

———

Extract from the Minutes of the Proceedings of the Bank Convention, held at New York on the 27th November to the 2d December 1837.

Present—Delegates of Banks from the following States, viz.: Maine, Vermont, New-Hampshire, Massachusetts, Rhode Island, Connecticut, New York, New Jersey, Pennsylvania, Delaware, District of Columbia, Virginia, North Carolina, South Carolina, Georgia, Ohio, Kentucky, and Indiana.

Thursday, November 30, 1837.

The Convention met according to adjournment.

Mr. Van Ness, from the committee appointed to report upon the proper measures to be pursued " to effect a general resumption of specie payments," &c. reported the following Resolutions, and requested that they should be considered a Report in part:

1st. *Resolved*, That it be recommended to the Banks of the several States to resume specie payments on the first day of July next, without precluding an earlier resumption on the part of such banks as may find it necessary or deem it proper.

2d. *Resolved*, That a committee of —— delegates be appointed, whose duty it shall be to correspond with the several banks, and to collect all the necessary information concerning their respective situations, and the rate of foreign exchanges, and who shall be authorised, if they deem it necessary, to call, on giving thirty days' notice, another meeting of this Convention, inviting the attendance of delegates from the banks of the States not represented at this meeting.

3d. *Resolved*, That (notwithstanding the foregoing resolutions) it will be the duty of each and every bank in the United States to resume specie payments at the earliest period when their own means and the state of the exchanges will enable them to do so with a proper regard to their own safety, and the interests of the community.

On motion of Mr. Eyre of Pennsylvania, the resolutions were laid on the table, to enable him to present a Report and Resolutions from a minority of the same committee.

Mr. Eyre then submitted the following Report and Resolutions :

The minority of the committee, to whom the resolution of Mr. Howard, of Maryland, was referred, submit the following Report and Resolutions, as expressing briefly their views upon the subject referred :

That they have proceeded in their deliberations upon the subject committed to them, under a deep sense of its momentous importance in relation to the particular interests represented in this Convention ; still more to the general welfare ; with unaffected respect to public expectation, and a thorough conviction that nothing can excuse the continuance of suspension after the necessity which demands it shall have ceased. It will not be denied that the banks are prompted by their own interest to a resumption at the earliest possible period, when it is known that since the month of May last, they have been steadily contracting their business to an unprecedented amount, and to the utmost limit short of general bankruptcy.

It will be conceded that the resumption, accompanied by a revival of confidence, to be more and more firmly reinstated, is demanded by every consideration of the public welfare ; and the banks, sustained as they have been in the face of penalties and forfeitures, by a candid, just and generous community, cannot fail to be alive to the duty of cultivating the favor, and regarding most respectfully the opinion and general expectation, of their fellow citizens. Nor can it be overlooked, that, as their justification is, and has been from the beginning, *necessity* and self-preservation, for the country as well as themselves, it will lose its force whenever the apprehended dangers are at an end.

It will be conceded that an efficient and maintained recurrence to specie payments requires a simultaneous action throughout the country, and it is admitted on all hands, that your resolves will be only advisory, not compulsory.

In order to this, the restoration of domestic exchanges to their natural and regular condition and action is indispensable, and this must mainly depend upon the ability of the Southern and Western States, for resumption is not a measure of mere volition.

It cannot, therefore, but be a matter of much regret, that in your deliberations, you are not assisted by the counsels of delegates from the important points of Louisiana, Mississippi, Alabama, Tennessee, and some other States.

Yet the ability of these States, and their willingness to concur and co-operate with you in every reasonable and judicious measure which you may recommend, cannot be questioned, although the want of certain information leaves you at a loss to know, with desirable precision, at what period, or to what amount, their staples, on which their ability depends, will be brought into activity.

In regard to the question of resumption, the first thing which presents itself to our consideration is, the *time* when it is to be attempted.

Shall it be now?

In the present condition of foreign and domestic exchanges, it is believed that an *immediate* resumption of specie payments is utterly impracticable; none, even the most sanguine, have ever been heard to impugn, or even to express doubt of the undeniable truth of this position. This measure will therefore be passed by.

Shall it then be at a future period, now to be fixed by this Convention?

Against such a measure, many objections exist in the minds of the minority of your committee, some of which will be stated.

No one can foretell with satisfactory probability, when our domestic exchanges will be restored to order and regularity.

It must depend upon the value and quantity of the staple products of the Southern and Western States, and the same dependence attaches to our foreign Exchanges.

Until our foreign debt shall have been reduced, the present high rate of exchange must necessarily continue; so long too, the demand for specie, for the purposes of remittances, must last, and while it lasts, the opening of your vaults would be to impair your means, and to drain the country of its specie to a ruinous extent. Again, to fix *now* a period of specie payments, would be to count with dangerous confidence upon speculative opinions and contingencies.

Who can assure us that, at a day not so remote as to be for that reason inadmissible, our foreign debt will be sufficiently liquidated to bring down exchange and check the exportation of specie?

Who can say what is to be the quantity or prices of our staples of this year's crop, in the foreign market?

There must be much allowance for the time necessary for getting them there, and for their sale also—much, too, as regards their value, to the vacillation of prices, and to the force of the foreign policy by which it has been attempted, and with too much success, to break them down.

Besides these considerations, we cannot but look with apprehension to the insufficiency of the domestic supply of bread stuffs.

That there will be a large importation is presumed, and to that extent your means will be impaired, the foreign debt kept stationary, or possibly increased. Again, if the reliance upon contingencies should embolden you to fix a day, and in it you should be disappointed, you will have repeated the distress occasioned by severe curtailment, without accomplishing the object proposed, and with certain ruin to many. You will shake public confidence in your disposition, or your ability, to its foundation.

How and when can you hope to restore it?

Again: In the interval which would elapse until the arrival of the period you may fix upon, may it not happen that in some instances there will be an expansion of circulation, which will aggravate public calamity? Then, too, may not the measure now under consideration tempt to large importation of foreign goods by your own merchants? May it not encourage the foreign manufacturer to force his goods upon the country, and glut the market? Either of these would necessarily keep you in a state of indebtedness proportionally, and to keep up the exchanges; nor is the ardent commercial spirit of enterprise round the Cape to China, &c. to be lost sight of.

Afford the specie, and it will be extended to a dangerous excess, for the temptation is great.

Again: If you fix an early day of resumption, you increase the hazard of disappointment. If you fix upon a distant day, may it not happen that you postpone resumption beyond the period when in justice you ought to have resumed ?

Finally : Are you prepared to dismiss the hope that Congress will aid in relieving the country ?

Entertaining these views, briefly expressed, but which your intelligence will carry out, the minority of the committee cannot advise the determination, at this time, of the precise period when the resumption of specie payments may be effected. Natural causes are in operation, which, by judicious action, you may assist, but you may retard their progress by rash and imprudent attempts to force them ; and you will, moreover, be able to assure yourselves and the public that the resumption, so anxiously desired by all, will be accomplished as soon as it is practicable, and *then* certainly.

In accordance with what has been said, the minority of your committee offer the following resolutions :

Resolved, That this Convention will appoint a committee of — delegates, to whom shall be confided the important trust of diligently inquiring, and deliberately judging, when the condition and circumstances of the country shall have been such as to justify an early resumption of specie payments by the banks, at a fixed period.

2d. That when the said committee shall, in the exercise of sound discretion, be satisfied that such period has arrived, it shall be their duty to make it known to the presiding officer of this Convention, and that it shall be his duty thereupon, to summon a meeting of this Convention, with due notice to its members, at —————, to the end that the measure of resumption may be promptly adopted.

Saturday, December 2d, 1837.

The Convention met, according to adjournment, when the following resolutions were adopted :

1st. *Resolved*, That the Convention entertains a deep anxiety and a firm determination to accomplish the resumption of specie payments at the earliest period when it may be permanently practicable.

2d. *Resolved*, That in the opinion of this Convention the present circumstances of the country are not such as to make it expedient or prudent now to fix a day for the resumption of specie payments.

3d. *Resolved*, That when the Convention terminates its present session, it shall be adjourned to meet in the city of New York, on the second Wednesday of April next, for the purpose of considering, and if practicable determining, upon the day when specie payments may be resumed.

4th. *Resolved*, That this Convention strongly recommends to all the banks in the United States to continue, by proper measures, to prepare themselves for a return to specie payments within the shortest practicable period, after the next meeting of the Convention.

5th. *Resolved*, That the banks in those States not now represented, be earnestly requested to send delegates to the adjourned meeting of this Convention, and that the several delegates from all the States be desired to procure all such information in regard to the condition of the banks in their respective States, as may be attainable.

———

At a meeting of the Officers of the Banks of the City of New-York, held on the 15th December, 1837—

The delegates appointed to represent the said Banks in the Convention of the Banks of the several States, which met at New-York, on the 27th of

November last, and on the following days, to the 1st of this month, made the following report. Whereupon it was

Resolved, That the said report be accepted and published.

PETER STAGG, *Chairman.*

W. M. VERMILYE, *Secretary.*

REPORT.

The delegates appointed to represent the Banks of the city of New-York, in the general Bank Convention, held in the said city, on the 27th of November, 1837, respectfully submit, together with a copy of the proceedings of the Convention, the following report, explanatory of their votes in that body:

The banks of the several States have been vested with the power, and, in most of the States, especially in that of New-York, with the exclusive privilege of issuing a paper currency, on the express condition, that they should at all times, and whenever the demand was made, redeem it in gold or silver, the only constitutional legal tender or currency, with which debts may be discharged. Nothing, therefore, but the inability to perform the condition, can justify a suspension of specie payments on the part of the Banks.

The immediate causes which thus compelled the banks of the city of New-York to suspend specie payments, on the 10th of May last, are well known. The simultaneous withdrawing of the large public deposits, and of excessive foreign credits, combined with the great and unexpected fall in the price of the principal article of our exports, with an import of corn and bread stuffs such as had never before occurred, and with the consequent inability of the country, particularly of the South-Western States, to make the usual and expected remittances, did, at one and the same time, fall principally and necessarily on the greatest commercial emporium of the Union. After a long and most arduous struggle, during which the banks, though not altogether unsuccessfully, resisting the imperative foreign demand for the precious metals, were gradually deprived of a great portion of their specie, some unfortunate incidents of a local nature, operating in concert with other previous exciting causes, produced distrust and panic, and finally one of those general runs, which, if continued, no banks that issue paper money payable on demand, can ever resist; and which soon put it out of the power of those of this city to sustain specie payments. The example was followed by the banks throughout the whole country, with as much rapidity as the news of the suspension in New-York reached them, without waiting for an actual run, and principally, if not exclusively, on the alleged grounds of the effects to be apprehended from that suspension. Thus, whilst the New-York city banks were almost drained of their specie, those in other places preserved the amount which they held before the final catastrophe.

If the share of blame, which may justly be imputed to the banks, be analyzed, it will be found to consist in their not having, at an early period, duly appreciated the magnitude of the impending danger, and taken, in time, the measures necessary to guard against it; in their want of firmness when the danger was more apparent and alarming; in yielding to the demands for increased, or continued bank facilities, instead of resolutely curtailing their loans, and lessening their liabilities. Whether the most acute foresight, and the most powerful exertions, could have enabled the banks to have averted the blow, is a question which we are not called upon to discuss.

Whatever explanations may be given concerning the past, since nothing but actual inability can be alleged as an excuse for having ceased to perform the express condition on which the privilege to issue a paper currency had been granted, it is equally obvious, that nothing can justify a protracted suspension, but the continued inability to resume and sustain specie payments. This principle is indeed so evident, that, as an abstract proposition, its correctness is universally admitted: and all agree in expressing their

" thorough conviction, that nothing can excuse the continuance of suspension, after the necessity which demands it shall have ceased." But, in enumerating the objections to an early resumption, or to fixing a day for it, the discussion was not confined to arguments derived from a supposed continued inability on the part of the banks to resume ; but an appeal was also made to considerations of presumed expediency, connected with the general situation of the country, and on which the simple fact of the ability of the banks to resume, and sustain specie payments, does not depend.

It is but too well known, that a general suspension of specie payments by the banks is not confined to them alone, but extends instantaneously to the whole community. As they had substituted their paper for the metallic currency, and as even the portion of specie which still circulated, disappears at once, when the general bank suspension takes place, the depreciated bank paper currency alone remains, both as the only medium of payment, and, by a necessary consequence, as the practical standard of value. Thus, by a strange anomaly, whilst the courts of law can consider nothing but gold or silver as the legal payment of debts, every individual, without exception, who is not compelled by process of law, or who does not resort to the tribunals for redress, pays all his debts with, and receives nothing in payment but, an irredeemable, depreciated currency. A general usage, openly at war with law, usurps its place ; and the few cases where the laws are enforced, are only exceptions to the universal practice. Instead of the permanent and uniform standard of value provided by the constitution, and by which all contracts were intended to be regulated, we have at once fifty different and fluctuating standards, agreeing only in one respect, that of impairing the sanctity of contracts. Even restrictive and penal laws are openly and daily violated with impunity, by every body, in circulating notes forbidden by law. It is impossible that such a state of things should not gradually demoralize the whole community ; that a general relaxation in the punctual and honorable fulfilment of obligations and contracts, should not take place ; that that which operates as a general relief law, should not be attended with the same baneful effects which have always attended positive laws of the same character ; and that, if the present illegal system be much longer continued, the commercial credit and prosperity of the country, and more particularly of this city, should not be deeply and permanently injured.

When we see such extensive, general, and, we may say, intolerable evils, flowing from a general suspension of specie payments by the banks, it is monstrous to suppose that, if they are able to resume, and sustain such payments, they should have any discretionary right to decide, or even to discuss, the question, whether a more or less protracted suspension is consistent with their own views of " the condition and circumstances of the country." There would be no limit to such supposed discretion. Thus, for instance, should the hope of a favorable action of Congress on the currency be still alleged as a motive for delay. would not this be tantamount to protracted suspension for an indefinite period of time ?

The banks are bound by the strongest legal and moral obligations to resume specie payments whenever they are able to maintain such payments. It is the paramount duty to which every other consideration must yield. Their ability to perform that duty is the only question which they have a right to discuss, and which they are bound to examine with the utmost care and candor.

Strictly speaking, the power to issue paper money should cease whenever the express condition on which the privilege was granted cannot be performed. It is only through the indulgence of the Legislature, and of the community, that the banks are still permitted, for a while, to continue their issues. If there be, indeed, any considerations affecting the general welfare, which can render the continuance of an irredeemable currency desirable, after the time when the banks are or shall think themselves able to resume specie payments, the application for a further protraction must come from the parties interested, and not from the banks; and it must be made, not to the banks, but to the Legislature.

It was urged, that some respectable merchants, here and in other places, were opposed to an early resumption. During the late trying crisis, some of the most respectable and solvent members of the commercial community might have been under the necessity of requiring some indulgence, at least in point of time. But there is not one of those honorable men, who would not think himself disgraced and degraded, if, after having obtained the requisite time, he delayed the fulfilment of his engagements a single day after he had become able to do so. That which they require from the banks is, therefore, unjust and unreasonable: for they ask them to do that, from which, in their own case, they would shrink; and which, if done by any one in his individual capacity, they would consider as disgraceful and dishonorable.

It was indeed insisted, that some of the general considerations to which we have alluded, made it dangerous for the banks to attempt to resume specie payments. We will advert to all the objections truly of that character; but deem it unnecessary to take further notice of that founded on an expected action of Congress, or to dwell on those clearly arising from local or particular interests, such as the want of extended bank accommodations, and the supposed facilities afforded by a protracted suspension for the collection of debts. Yet, we must not be understood as admitting that such protraction would, in any respect, be advantageous to the community at large; believing, on the contrary, as we do, that its general and permanent interests would be sacrificed to temporary ease and particular classes, should the suspension be continued any longer than absolute necessity requires.

Amongst the considerations deemed by us to be irrelevant to the true and only question before the banks, that most strongly urged was the alleged necessity of a previous " restoration of domestic exchanges to their natural and regular condition and order." This is confounding cause and effect. The obligation to pay specie, is the check which regulates the exchanges and prevents them from rising much above the specie par. The suspension of specie payments, and the consequent great difference in value, as compared with specie, of the several local bank currencies, are the cause of the great corresponding inequalities of the domestic exchanges, so justly complained of; and the evil cannot otherwise be overcome, than by a general resumption of specie payments. If A, in Philadelphia, is obliged to lose ten per cent., in order to draw his funds from Nashville, it is because (whether owing to excess in circulation, or to great indebtedness, is immaterial) the Tennessee bank currency is worth ten per cent. less than that of Philadelphia. If specie payments were resumed in both places, he would lose, at most, two or three per cent. on the exchange. But A is now permitted, by general usage, to pay his debts at home in Philadelphia bank paper, worth six per cent. less than specie. He apprehends that, if the Philadelphia banks should resume specie payments before those of Tennessee, being obliged to pay his own debts in paper equal to specie, he would lose 16, instead of 10 per cent., on the Tennessee exchange. The argument, derived from the present condition of domestic exchanges, resolves itself, therefore, into one of expediency. It is founded on the inadmissible supposition, that in order to accommodate special interests, and to benefit certain classes, the banks, though, from their situation and resources, able to resume specie payments, have a right to protract the suspension, to postpone the payment of their own debts, and to delay the performance of the paramount duty they owe to the community at large, of restoring a currency equal to gold or silver.

The only question, on which the convention was called upon to deliberate, being the ability of the banks to resume and sustain specie payments, it appeared to the delegates of both the city and country banks of New York, that an early day might at this time be designated for that purpose.

In their first circular of the 18th of August, the committee of correspondence of the city banks had pointed out such a favorable alteration in the rate of foreign exchanges, as would remove the danger of an immediate exportation of the precious metals, and a concert on the part of the principal banks of the country, as the only requisites for resuming with safety.

In reference to the first point, several estimates of the amount of foreign debt still due, neither provided for, nor postponed, and which probably would be demanded, and must be paid, before the first of July next, were alluded to in the course of the discussion. Those estimates varied from five to twenty millions of dollars. The lowest calculation appeared to rest on correct data : but if somewhat too low, the difference might be readily provided for, by the first proceeds of the cotton crop, and by the sale of State stocks. But it was not at all·necessary to resort to calculations of the amount of our foreign debt. Its effect on foreign exchanges, and on a consequent drain of specie for exportation, is the only point in which the banks are concerned, and which could affect the question under consideration.

At the very time when the convention was deliberating, the exchange on London, which had been as high as 121, had fallen to 114, nominal ; and the true par being a fraction above $109\frac{1}{2}$ nominal, the exchange was in fact but four per cent. above par in city bank paper. But that paper was itself at five per cent. below specie; and the rate of exchange was, therefore, one per cent. below specie par. In other words, any given quantity of New York bank notes could purchase bills on London, exceeding by one per cent. the corresponding amount in specie which the same quantity of bank notes could purchase. Ninety-nine gold sovereigns cost as much as a bill on London of one hundred pounds sterling. Under such circumstances, specie could not be exported without a loss, and accordingly the exportation had altogether ceased. It is well known that, within a week after the adjournment of the convention, a further fall had reduced the rate of exchange to $111\frac{1}{2}$ nominal; that is to say, to $2\frac{1}{2}$ per cent. below the true specie par, and within less than 2 per cent. of being at par with New York bank notes. But, reverting to the time when the convention was sitting, the requisite alteration was no longer a matter of conjecture; and the fact, that the exchange had fallen below the true specie par, and that the exportation of specie had ceased, had actually taken place.

Apprehensions were nevertheless expressed, of the effect which large importations of grain and merchandise might hereafter have on the foreign exchanges, and of an expected drain of specie for the China trade. It appeared to us, that if, after the principal acknowledged cause of the suspension, and which presented the greatest obstacle to the resumption, had actually ceased to operate, we were permitted to allege conjectures and contingencies, as a proper ground for protracting the suspension, there was no time at which some plausible reasons of a similar character might not be adduced, and the resumption be indefinitely postponed.

With respect to the danger of excessive importations, it might indeed be apprehended that, whenever the pressure of the foreign debt was removed, the commercial community might, with its characteristic energetic spirit of enterprise, resume its business too soon, and on too large a scale. And it is, on that account, highly important, that the banks should seize eagerly that eventful moment, and, as it may be called, the turn of the tide, for an immediate resumption, before new undertakings may raise new obstacles to the accomplishment of that object.

The danger of unfavorable exchanges, and of an extraordinary exportation of specie, being now out of question, what other causes could impair the ability of the banks, generally, or in some sections of the country, to resume specie payments within a very short period?

The four great South-Western States were not represented in the convention: and it will be admitted that some of them may not be ready as early as the other parts of the Union. It is, on that point, sufficient to observe, 1st. That, being largely debtors, their not resuming immediately cannot in any way affect the stability of specie payments by the other States. 2d. That the resumption by other States will not, in the slightest degree, impair the productive industry of those districts, whose great natural resources will, notwithstanding the peculiar situation of their banks, early and powerfully promote the payment of debts and the renewal of sound business.

By no other portion of the country was it intimated, that there were any banks whose particular situation required a longer time than might be wanted by those of New York: unless this should have been implied in some allusions to the respective indebtedness to each other, of the several cities or districts. In such cases, justice requires, and it may be done in a very short time, that the necessary curtailments should be made in the debtor places, and the resources thus obtained should be applied to the discharge of such debts, and, when necessary, to the purchase of specie. This is, in fact, the course pointed out by the resolution, unanimously adopted by the convention: "That this convention strongly recommends to all the banks of the United States, to continue, by proper measures, to prepare themselves to return to specie payments, within the shortest practicable period after the next meeting of the convention."

We have every reason to believe, that the banks represented in the convention were in a sound state; and, in every respect, as well prepared and able to resume specie payments as those of the city of New York. It would indeed be strange that it should be otherwise. New York suffered incomparably more than any other city; the failures were far more numerous; its banks were subject more than any others to the causes which produced the suspension, and alone to a run of domestic origin, alone drained of the greater part of their specie, whilst banks in other places preserved the greater part of theirs.

The only reason which remains to be examined, is the apprehension that confidence may not have been sufficiently restored to ensure a permanent resumption. The causes which occasioned the distrust, the panic, and the run on some of the banks, have ceased to operate. Such coincidence of extraordinary events and unfortunate incidents, as produced the catastrophe, must be rare, and may never again occur. It must be conceded, that it is impossible that confidence should be restored, until the banks shall have resumed specie payments, or designated an early day for that purpose. Combined with the conviction of the ability of the banks to resume, and with the fact that their paper shall have become equal, or nearly equal, in value to specie, nothing is wanted for restoring entire confidence, but the simultaneous resumption by the principal banks, acting in concert.

Although the convention could not be prevailed upon, either to fix at this time a day on which to resume, or to meet again on an earlier day than the 11th of April; although it is peculiarly to be regretted that, from incidental considerations, it should not have yielded to our request to meet in the first days of March; yet the conference has been attended with considerable advantages. There has been a free and mutual interchange of opinions. The serious attention of all the banks has been drawn to the absolute necessity of an early resumption; and the suggestion of a postponement for an indefinite time, if ever seriously entertained, has been abandoned. We may now rely with confidence on a great unanimity from the Eastern, Southern, and North-Western sections of the Union, in fixing, at our next meeting, the earliest practicable day for the resumption of specie payments. It is true that the banks of Philadelphia and Baltimore appeared to contemplate a more remote time than we did, not certainly because of being less able or prepared than ourselves, or others, but on general grounds. It now appears, from official returns, that the banks of Pennsylvania are, in every respect, better prepared than those of the city of New York. And it has been announced by the highest authority in that State, that "the banks of Pennsylvania are in a much sounder state than before the suspension; and that the resumption of specie payments, so far as it depends on their situation and resources, may take place at any time." The great fall at this early day in the rate of foreign exchanges, which has exceeded our most sanguine expectations, had not been anticipated by them. A fact so important, and which gives a new aspect to the whole subject, cannot fail to have a powerful influence on their decision. We entertain sanguine hopes, that this and the course of events will remove their objections, and induce them to unite and act in concert with us. We are under the firm conviction, that the result depends on their determination, and that, if they agree to it, the resumption may with facility be effected at an early day. Should they persevere in the opinion, that an early resumption is inexpedient and dangerous, it may, considering the magnitude of their capital, prove difficult for the other banks, and particularly for those of this city, with their resources alone, to maintain permanently specie payments.

In the meanwhile, the line of our duty is obvious: and we have only to continue, by every measure in our power, to strengthen ourselves, and to be prepared, at the earliest possible day, to fulfil our engagements, and to resume and maintain specie payments. To the early completion of the measures now in train for that purpose, we respectfully, but most earnestly call the immediate attention of the city banks, as an indispensable requisite before a day can be fixed for resumption. The country banks, with most laudable exertions, have taken all the necessary steps, and are prepared to resume at any time.

> ALBERT GALLATIN,
> GEO. NEWBOLD,
> C. W. LAWRENCE,
> CORNS. HEYER,
> JOHN J. PALMER,
> PRESERVED FISH.
> G. A. WORTH.

December 15, 1837.

At a meeting of the officers of the banks of the city of New York, held on the 28th of February, 1838, the committee on the "resumption of specie payments" submitted the following Report in part, viz.:

In contemplation of the resumption of specie payments, by the banks of the city of New York, on or before the tenth day of May next, and under the uncertain condition of a simultaneous or early resumption by the banks of some of the other great commercial cities, it is incumbent on those of New York to adopt all the measures, within the limits of their resources, which may enable them not only to resume, but also to maintain, specie payments.

Much has already been done in that respect, the result as well of causes not under the control of the banks, as of positive action on their part.

1. It appears by the annual returns of the Bank Commissioners that, exclusively of the Dry Dock Bank, which is not included in the return of this year, the gross amount of all the liabilities of the city banks, payable on demand,

deducting therefrom the notes and checks of other banks held by them, and the balances due to them by other banks, amounted,

On the 1st of January, 1836, to $26,918,105
"   "   1837, to 25,485,287
"   "   1838, to 12,920,694

making a diminution in the liabilities of more than twelve millions and a half during the year 1837.

2. The detailed statement for the 1st of January, 1838, rendered by the several city banks to their standing committee, shows a balance to their credit of more than four millions, due to them by banks out of the State, and of more than two millions in account with all the banks out of the city. Ample means, as also appears by those statements, have been provided by the country banks of the State, for the redemption of their notes which circulate in the city.

On a view of the whole subject, we may confidently say, that the relative strength of the banks is, and at the time of the resumption will be, greater than it was during the last two years, and probably at any former time.

The fall in the rate of foreign exchanges, now considerably below par in our city paper, renders it absolutely certain that no exportation of specie can take place, and more than probable that a considerable influx may be expected. This fact, now indisputable, must have an effect on public opinion, and ought to remove the apprehensions of those who may have believed our efforts for an early resumption premature. Secure, as all the banks in the United States are, against foreign demands, we are justified in expecting their co-operation. If this is obtained, we do not perceive any obstacle to an early, easy and safe resumption of specie payments.

A continued suspension, on the part of some of the other great commercial cities, can alone render the resumption on our part difficult, and may prevent a free application of the legitimate banking resources of New York. Yet such is the favorable relative state of the balances between this and the other parts of the Union, that, for the present at least, but little need be apprehended from the effect of natural causes. Of deliberate acts of hostility, as there could be no motive for such, there should be no apprehension on our part. We trust that, supported by the community of the city and by this State, the banks will be able to surmount all obstacles, and, on or before the tenth of May, to resume and maintain specie payments.

The preparatory measures on their part appear to be, 1st, a reduction of their liabilities out of the State, and drawing in their foreign funds; 2d, an equalization of the balances due to and from each other, and a mutual return of their notes, which may enable all to resume on an equal footing and with equal safety; 3d, a sufficient increase of their specie. On these points the committee will submit a separate report.

Signed,   ALBERT GALLATIN,
PETER STAGG,
GEO. NEWBOLD,
CORNS. HEYER,
JOHN J. PALMER,
C. W. LAWRENCE,
F. W. EDMONDS.

Whereupon, the report was unanimously adopted by the meeting.
On motion, *Resolved*, That the same be published.
Signed,   BENJ. M. BROWN, *Chairman.*
W. M. VERMILYE, *Secretary.*

Extract from the Minutes of the Proceedings of the adjourned meeting of the Bank Convention, held at New York, on the 11th to the 16th April, 1838.

Present—Delegates of banks from the following States, viz. : Maine, Vermont, New Hampshire,* Massachusetts, Rhode Island, Connecticut, New York, New Jersey, Delaware, Maryland,* District of Columbia, Virginia, North Carolina, Indiana, Illinois, Missouri, Mississippi, and from Pittsburgh, (Pennsylvania.)†

The following letter, among others, was placed upon the minutes of the Convention:

Philadelphia, April 4th, 1838.

Sir,—At a meeting, held this day, of committees from all the banks of the city and liberties of Philadelphia, a notice was received from you of the adjourned meeting of the Convention of Banks, to be held at New York on the 11th of this month. The banks of Philadelphia having declined to send delegates to that adjourned meeting, I have been instructed to apprise you of their determination, and, as a just mark of respect to the Convention, as well as to yourself personally, to state the reasons of their absence. This duty I hasten to perform.

On the 19th of August 1837, an invitation was given to the banks of Philadelphia, in behalf of the banks of the city of New York, to meet in convention at the city of New York, " for the purpose of agreeing on the time when specie payments should be resumed, and on the measures to effect that purpose." The reason assigned for the invitation was, that " it would be impracticable for those of any particular section to resume, without a general explanation of at least the principal banks of the great ports of the country ; a mutual and free communication of their respective situations, prospects, and opinions, seem to be a necessary preliminary step." To this the banks of Philadelphia answered on the 29th of August, stating their belief that " the general resumption of specie payments depends mainly, if not exclusively, on the action of Congress, the body charged with the general power over commerce, and the exclusive power over the coinage ; and, without whose co-operation, all attempts at a general system of payments in coin, throughout this extensive country, must be partial and temporary ;" and they concluded with a declaration, " that it is inexpedient at this time to appoint delegates to the proposed Convention."

At a subsequent period, on the 21st of October 1837, a second invitation was received from the banks of the city of New York, for a similar meeting on the 27th of November. Although entertaining precisely the same opinions as to the inexpediency of any resumption, without previously understanding the intentions of the Government, the banks of Philadelphia are yet unwilling to do any thing which might seem to be discourteous to the banks of the city of New York, and accordingly sent delegates to the Convention. After remaining in session for a week, that body was unable to name any day for the resumption ; but adjourned to meet again the 11th of April, " for the purpose of considering. and if practicable, determining upon the day when specie payments may be resumed;" at the same time resolving, " that the banks in those States not now represented, be earnestly requested to send delegates to the adjourned meeting of this Convention ; and that the several delegates from all the States be desired to procure all such information in regard to the condition of the banks in their respective States, as may be attainable."

On the 26th of January, a delegation from the banks of the city of New-

---

* The delegates from Maryland and New Hampshire withdrew.
† And those from Pittsburgh declined voting on the final question.

York visited Philadelphia, and while there addressed a letter to the Philadelphia banks, stating that they were desirous of ascertaining "if the Philadelphia banks will agree with them to name a day, not later than the period mentioned, (May,) when they will simultaneously adopt the same measure."

To this the Philadelphia banks answered, on the 31st of January, stating, that "It is undoubtedly true, that any resumption, to be easy, must be simultaneous; and, to be effectual, must be general. Nor is it less true, that a partial resumption, by any party to the Convention, must derange the relations of the whole to each other, and disturb the preparations which all are making to produce an uniform result at the period fixed by the Convention. The banks of Philadelphia, therefore, consider it scarcely just or respectful to the banks of other States, whose co-operation was in the first instance invited, to take any steps in opposition to what was settled by the Convention, without full concert with the other members of that body, who separated under conviction that no action would take place on a matter so important to their interests, until they were re-assembled;" and added, "on a careful consideration of all these circumstances, the banks of Philadelphia think it premature to name any day for the resumption of specie payments until the adjourned meeting of the Convention."

Soon after the return of that delegation, the banks of the city of New York published, on the 28th of February, a declaration, that, "in contemplation of the resumption of specie payments by the banks of the city of New York, on or before the tenth of May next, and under the uncertain contingency of a simultaneous or early resumption by the banks of some of the other great commercial cities, it is incumbent on those of New York to adopt all the measures, within the limits of their resources, which may enable them not only to resume, but also to maintain, specie payments." And immediately a general meeting of the citizens of New York adopted the following resolution: "That this meeting hails with great satisfaction, the declarations, on the part of the New York city banks, of their purpose to resume specie payments on or before the 10th of May next."

From this review it is manifest, that the convention contemplated was one embracing delegates from every part of the Union; meeting in good faith to confer on subjects of equal interest to them all; exchanging opinions frankly; giving information as to the conditions of the respective sections they represented, so as to fix some scheme of action which might unite all interests, and combine all efforts. That was the design of the original meeting of the convention—that ought to be the object of the adjourned meeting. It was, therefore, seen with equal surprise and regret, that the banks of New York announced their determination to resume on a day named. This was done without waiting for the meeting of the delegates, which they had themselves invited to New York. It was done in obvious opposition to the spirit of consultation and inquiry, which were presumed to be the whole purpose of the convention. It was done in disregard of the friendly but decided opinion of the Philadelphia banks, that it would be neither just nor courteous to act until the convention were re-assembled. Of the propriety of this determination by the banks of the city of New York, the banks of Philadelphia do not presume to offer an opinion. But it is manifest, that this decision gives an entirely new character to the convention. The party who convoke the assembly to confer with the other banks on the several interests of all, has, without waiting for their arrival, decided the question exclusively in reference to his own peculiar interests. It meets them to discuss what is already settled; and the only point which remains will be, not whether the banks of New York and the banks of all the other States should resume specie payments, but simply, whether the banks of the city of New York having decided to resume specie payments on a day named, the banks of the other States must do the same. In that question the banks of Philadelphia desire to take no part. They do not wish to give any advice in regard to the course which the banks of the city of New York have resolved to pursue; they do not wish to receive any from those banks touching their own course. Accordingly, they deem it better to abstain altogether from a meeting in which their delegates can no longer find an appropriate place.

I need scarcely add, that this determination implies not the slightest want of respect to the convention, or to its highly respectable presiding officer, but is founded exclusively on consideration of duty to themselves, and to the general interests of the country.

I have the honor to be, very respectfully,

Signed,   W. MEREDITH, *Chairman.*

SAMUEL HUBBARD, ESQ.
President of the Convention.

Attest, T. B. TREVOR, *Secretary.*

At a meeting of the association of the delegates of the banks of the city of Philadelphia and districts, held on the 4th day of April 1838, the following resolutions were adopted:

Resolved, That it is inexpedient to send delegates to the adjourned meeting at New York, of the bank convention, on the 11th of this month.

Resolved, That the following letter be transmitted by the chairman of this meeting to the president of that convention, to explain the reasons of the absence of the delegates from Philadelphia.

Extract from the Minutes:

J. B. TREVOR, *Secretary.*

On motion of Mr. Brockenbrough of Virginia, it was

Resolved, That the correspondence furnished to the convention, by Mr. Newbold of New York, with the Secretary of the Treasury, be placed upon the minutes of the proceedings of this convention.

(COPY.)

[PRIVATE.]   Bank of America, April 7, 1838.

Dear Sir,—So much is said in the public press, and daily repeated elsewhere, of the hostile disposition of the Government towards the Banks, and of the measures in contemplation by the Treasury Department, calculated, it is said, to injure and embarrass the Banks, and to retard, if not prevent, their resumption of specie payments, that I am induced to address you on the subject. Not, however, that any thing is necessary to satisfy me that those assertions and assumptions are wholly unfounded; but that you may, if you shall deem it expedient and proper, take measures to correct the misrepresentations and remove the fears and apprehensions that they may have excited in the community, and especially in the minds of many honest and honorable men.

It is loudly and confidently asserted, and widely and industriously circulated, that the measures that will be pursued by the Treasury in the collection and disbursement of the public money, will render it difficult for the Banks to resume and maintain specie payments. Fears and apprehensions are thus excited, confidence impaired, and the best efforts of the banks are in some degree paralyzed. Designing men avail of this state of things to promote and affect their special purposes, and industry and talent are not wanting to make their efforts essentially mischievous. Permit me, therefore, to ask whether there is no way by which the mischief may be abated and successfully counteracted. Of this you will best judge and determine yourself. My present object is more immediately in reference to the approaching convention of Bank Delegates to be held in this city, on the 11th inst.; and being satisfied that efforts will there be made to impress the belief, that the fears and apprehensions alluded to are well founded, and that it would therefore be unsafe and inexpedient for the Banks to fix a day for the resumption of specie payments. I consider it to be of the utmost importance that such efforts should be effectively met, and that all unfounded suspicions and suggestions should be removed or successfully confronted. I beg, therefore, respectfully to suggest for your consideration, whether you will not be pleased to enable and authorise me to communicate to the convention, if it shall be necessary, your views and wishes on the subject of the resumption of specie payments, and the course, or probable course, of the Treasury in reference to the Banks, after they shall have resumed. It is an important crisis for this city and this State—indeed for the whole Union; and being anxious to do every thing in my power to promote and accomplish the right result—a general resumption of specie payments—I am sure that you will excuse me for these suggestions, be your conclusions respecting them what they may.

I am, with great respect, dear sir, your obedient servant.

Signed, GEORGE NEWBOLD.

Hon. Levi Woodbury, *Secretary Treasury U. S.*
Washington.

Treasury Department, 9th April, 1838.

Sir,—I have to acknowledge the receipt of your letter of the 7th inst. In order that you may fully understand the views and wishes entertained by this department, on the subject of a resumption of specie payments by the Banks, and the course to be pursued by the Treasury towards them, I herewith enclose copies of two private letters written some weeks since in answer to inquiries similar to yours.

It is only necessary to add, that the same views are still cherished, and that the notes of specie-paying banks at par where offered, are now received for duties, and will undoubtedly continue to be. They are and will be paid out when acceptable to the public creditors, and no accumulation of them beyond our current expenditures is anticipated at any point whatever during the present or ensuing year.

I am, sir, very respectfully, your obedient servant,

Signed, LEVI WOODBURY.

George Newbold, Esq., *President of the Bank of America.*

Washington, 18th March, 1838.

Dear Sir,—In reply to yours of the 14th inst., I hasten to remark, that the Treasury Department has long been anxious as yourself and many others, for the resumption of specie payments by the banks. All has been and will be done by it, which comes within its limited powers, to promote, at the earliest day possible, so desirable an event.

I do not hesitate to say fully and frankly, that the impression is altogether erroneous, that specie is to be purchased and hoarded by the Government. Only a few thousand dollars of it have yet been raised on Treasury Notes, and none is intended to be hereafter, except to the extent needed to supply the current demands of the Government. Whatever may be thus obtained or received for public dues of any kind, will be forthwith paid out again to defray the appropriations; and the settled policy of the Department has been, and will be, to keep nothing idle in the Treasury, while the power exists to issue Treasury Notes to meet contingencies and deficiencies, as they may hereafter occur. Respectfully yours,

Signed, LEVI WOODBURY.

Nathan Appleton, Esq.
Boston, Mass.

Washington, March 18, 1838.

Dear Sir,—In reply to yours of the 16th inst., I hasten to remove any erroneous inferences from the rumor mentioned.

The settled policy of the Department, and one which it makes known to all inquirers, is to promote the resumption of specie payments by the banks, so far as its limited powers may permit.

Consequently it has not, and will not hereafter, purchase specie, beyond what may be needed for immediate disbursements; and in that way will neither hoard it nor compete with others for its possession.

All we receive in any way will immediately be paid out again to defray appropriations.

I make these statements explicitly and promptly, and have forwarded similar ones to Boston, in order that no injurious apprehensions need be entertained as to the financial operations of the Government.

Respectfully yours,

LEVI WOODBURY.

J. D. BEERS, ESQ.
    New York City.

Friday, April 13th, 1838.

Mr. Ware of Maine, from the committee of one for each State, made the following report:

That said committee have adopted the following resolutions, which they recommend to the convention for consideration and adoption, viz.:

Resolved, That it be recommended to all the banks of the several States, to resume specie payments on the first Monday in October next, without precluding an earlier resumption on the part of such banks as may find it necessary or deem it proper.

Resolved, That it is important to the success of the effort to return to specie payments, and to restore the currency to a sound condition, that the banks should be sustained by the General Government.

Monday, April 16th, 1838.

The Convention proceeded to the consideration of the Report and Resolutions, when Mr. Brockenbrough, of Virginia, moved to amend the same, by striking out all after the word "Report," and insert in lieu thereof the following:

Whereas, it is found necessary, in order to simultaneous action by the banks, in the resumption of specie payments, so to proceed in designating a period for that purpose as to secure the nearest approach to unanimity; and whereas, whilst, in the judgment of this Convention, the return to specie payments, and preservation of the currency in a sound condition, will depend essentially on the course of the General Government, yet this Convention regards it as the duty of the banks to make the effort in good faith, exclusive of any direct reference to the prospective measures of the Government. At the same time, the Convention has been happy to observe, in recent letters of the Secretary of the Treasury, specific assurances of an intention to sustain the banks, so far as it may be done through the fiscal operations of that department of the Government.*

Resolved, That it be recommended to all the banks of the several States to resume specie payments on the first day of January next, without precluding

---

* The allusions to the course of the General Government referred principally to the threatened Sub-Treasury plan, which was considered as hostile to the banks which intended to resume specie payments.

an earlier resumption on the part of such banks as may find it necessary or deem it proper.

Which Preamble and Resolution were adopted by the Convention.

[The banks of New York, finding that a majority of the Convention was against a general resumption so early as May, had only requested that, at least, the day recommended should be the 1st of July. This was refused; they resumed alone on the 10th of May; and, although the Convention had thought it unsafe to recommend an earlier day than the 1st of January, 1839, public opinion compelled almost all the banks to resume in July.]

Letters written in 1830, *relating to Mr. Gallatin's subsequent Pamphlet on Currency, published the same year.*

New York, 27th April, 1830.

To ROBERT WALSH, Jr., *Philadelphia:*

Dear Sir,—It is doubtful whether I will have time to prepare, in season, such an article in relation to *currency* as you desire, and still more so, whether I can write any thing on that subject worthy of the public, and corresponding with your views. So much has been written on that question, that it does not seem to me that anything new can be advanced, in support of what are admitted, by almost all enlightened and disinterested men, to be correct principles. The only points at all dubious, at least in my opinion, are those of *local currencies*, or what is commonly called " country notes," and of the simultaneous circulation of gold and silver. Was it practicable, the following outline would appear to me preferable to any other, as combining safety, convenience and facilities sufficient to promote industry and prudent enterprise:

1. No other but the Bank of the United States, nor any individual, associations or corporations, to be permitted to issue any bank notes, bills of credit, or paper, in the nature of currency; but all such bank or bankers to be left, without restrictions or special tax, at liberty to pursue, in other respects, their proper occupation, viz.: to receive deposits, to discount notes, and to deal in bills of exchange or bullion; thereby assimilating them to the bankers of London, and to all those of the continent of Europe; neither of whom issue a single shilling of paper currency.

2. The Bank of the United States to issue no notes of a denomination under *one hundred dollars*, (a restriction the same as that of the Bank of France,) those of a lower denomination excepted, which it may make redeemable at whichever of its offices they may be presented for payment.

3. Gold and silver United States coins to circulate, either on the new British plan of issuing silver at *ten* or *fifteen* per cent. above its intrinsic value, but not to be a legal tender for sums above ten dollars; or simultaneously for all purposes, but rating gold at its true value, which may be done so near the true ratio of gold to silver (about 15·6 to 1) as to obviate every practical objection.

4. All foreign coins to be excluded; copper coins to remain as now, but not to be a legal tender for more than *fifty* cents.

You may perceive that I am an ultra-bullionist, which it is right you should know. But I am perfectly sensible, that Congress will not attempt to prohibit the issue of notes by State banks; that we have no other security against their over-issues but State laws, which some States will not enact, and the Bank of the United States; that our reliance for a sound currency, and therefore for a just performance of contracts, rests on that institution; and that, in order to enable it to check and counteract the evil tendency of the local currencies, it must be permitted to issue notes of a smaller denomination than would otherwise be eligible. The principal object at this time is to preserve what we have, rather than to aim at what cannot be obtained. But I know too well, from sad experience, how difficult it is, without the aid of party, to carry any measure however useful, which is opposed from sectional or interested views. And yet, though aware of the unavailing effect of argument under such circumstances, I would be disposed to contribute my mite, if I thought I could add any thing to what has been done by others. It is also so long since my mind was made up on the subject, that I have not lately collected any facts. The evidence reported by the committees of both Houses of Parliament, previous to the resuming of specie payments in Great Britain, is the last document of any importance which I read with attention. A correct statement of the amount and nature of our currency is an indispensable preliminary to any essay on the subject. The ordinary returns of the Bank of the United States and of the several State banks, of the latest dates that can be obtained, not in the aggregate for each State, but showing the situation of each bank, would be sufficient, as I am familiar with those returns. The cashiers of the several offices of the Bank of the United States might with ease procure most of them. If you can obtain these for me, I will try to write, with the understanding that, if prevented or not satisfied myself, I will put my notes in your hands, to be used as you may think proper. I have, &c.

ALBERT GALLATIN.

New York, 22d May, 1830.

To the Hon. G. C. VERPLANCK, M. C., *Washington*:

Dear Sir,—I have been much gratified by the Report of the Committee of Ways and Means on the Bank of the United States, which I think to be the ablest paper that has issued this session, from any committee of either house. The constitutional question is treated with great ability, and placed on the most solid ground that could have been selected. I would, indeed, be inclined to go farther than the committee, and to insist that the term "bill of credit" in the constitution, embraces every species of paper currency, and therefore precludes the issuing of bank notes under State authority. That a purely metallic currency would be preferable to one hundred independent local paper currencies, is indisputable; and considering the perpetual tendency manifested everywhere, by every Government or public institution, to abuse the power of issuing paper, it is at least doubtful, whether it would not be safer to abstain altogether from issuing that dangerous instrument as currency. Admitting this to be impracticable, I cannot, though aware of the objections to a powerful monied institution, perceive any better check against over-issues, or any other security for preserving a proper standard of value, than the Bank of the United States, or at least one founded on the same principles.

There are, however, some positions in the report, to which, as now informed, I cannot yield an unqualified assent.

I was, at the time, of opinion, that specie payments might have been restored in 1815, without the establishment of the bank (a), although that institution gave the best practicable security against a recurrence of the evil.

(a) I might have added, that, though not then in office, I strongly urged in the autumn of 1815, the adoption of such measures as might have effected the object; funding the excess of Treasury Notes afloat, and receiving no notes of suspended banks in payment of duties and taxes, or of public lands.

I also think that the depreciation of a paper currency does not exclusively depend on, or always correspond with, its excess; and that this depreciation does not occasion that of a simultaneously circulating metallic currency; and although I am an ultra-bullionist, it seems to me that the loss arising from the suspension of specie payments, which was incurred by Government during the war, is overrated in the report. But on those and some other points connected with the general question of currency, to which I have paid great attention, I only wish to be enlightened; and the principal object of this letter is to request you to have the goodness to supply me, if in your power, with such further documents as may throw light on the subject. I can at present only point out the following, to which you may add such other as you may think useful, and are within your reach.

1. The Report itself with the annexed tables.
2. Mr. Crawford's Report of 1820, therein alluded to.
3. The Report of the Committee of the Senate of this session on the Bank of the United States.
4. The Report (dates not recollected, 1813 to 1817] showing the amount respectively subscribed in the several States, &c. to the loans obtained during the war.
5. The Report, or Reports, showing the amount of Treasury Notes issued during the war, their redemption by funding or payment, with the dates of such issues and redemption.
6. The late Report of the Secretary of the Treasury to the Senate respecting the relative value of gold and silver.

I think that the immediate causes which produced the suspension of specie payments, are not sufficiently investigated in the report. Excessive issues of bank notes, and perhaps withdrawing of specie, will be the answer. But what was the cause of those excessive issues, which had not operated, for the three years immediately following the dissolution of the first Bank of the United States? This is an important question, as connected with the degree of security afforded by the present Bank against another suspension in time of war, and with the extent to which it may at such time afford or promote the loans wanted by Government. A knowledge of the precise situation of the principal banks in June 1812, and when they stopt payment in specie, would materially assist in discovering the immediate cause of that event.

I am, &c.

ALBERT GALLATIN.

123

Resources and Liabilities of the Banks in the different divisions of the Union.

NEAR MAY, 1837.

	Discounts, Loans, Stocks and other investments.	Specie.	Notes of other Banks, & other Specie Funds.	Balance due by other Banks.	Balance due to other Banks.	Gross amount of Circulation.	Deposits.	Other Liabilities.
Eastern	99,563,979	2,550,477	5,365,843	2,506,964	—	19,674,994	14,242,806	8,529,832
New-York	79,120,069	3,109,209	7,025,645	1,790,006	—	15,953,177	23,745,374	9,525,862
Middle	85,117,901	5,216,914	7,254,808	—	1,709,969	21,228,114	22,161,066	6,923,609
Unied States Bank	69,867,780	1,490,968	2,689,470	—	333,601	7,193,021	2,921,969	11,494,149
Southern	62,122,038	6,468,971	2,669,030	25,514	—	23,451,850	13,202,752	1,380,960
South-Western	121,470,313	4,277,468	2,465,900	—	7,528,062	19,159,924	19,380,845	9,152,529
North-Western	45,685,609	6,698,896	3,437,446	3,690,815	—	16,907,107	15,356,069	2,409,690
Total	562,967,689	29,812,903	30,808,142	8,013,299	9,571,632	123,628,087	111,010,881	49,416,631

NEAR MAY, 1838.

	Discounts, Loans, Stocks and other investments.	Specie.	Notes of other Banks, & other Specie Funds.	Balance due by other Banks.	Balance due to other Banks.	Gross amount of Circulation.	Deposits.	Other Liabilities.
Eastern	89,673,140	3,252,663	4,041,217	810,565	—	19,422,116	8,178,989	5,022,556
New-York	63,135,944	9,357,495	8,289,871	13,146	—	12,934,652	18,451,860	7,510,025
Middle	74,370,557	6,292,829	6,025,629	3,064,934	4,898,682	19,024,642	19,961,310	7,808,260
Unied States Bank	72,548,842	4,409,330	1,611,072	—	—	6,451,605	4,414,978	18,121,440
Southern	58,410,803	6,933,341	4,604,686	1,805,148	—	22,845,721	10,151,411	4,790,431
South-Western	140,379,675	5,413,648	2,899,157	—	10,557,649	29,104,279	18,979,641	12,487,779
North-Western	45,206,726	8,505,598	3,383,391	3,889,952	—	17,481,100	9,086,648	3,486,147
Total	543,725,667	44,164,904	30,855,023	9,583,745	15,456,331	127,294,115	89,224,837	59,226,638

The Eastern Division embraces the States of Maine, New Hampshire, Vermont, Rhode Island, and Connecticut.
The Middle includes New Jersey, Pennsylvania, Delaware, Maryland, and the District of Columbia.
The Southern,—Virginia, North Carolina, South Carolina, Georgia, and the Territory of Florida.
The South-Western,—Alabama, Mississippi, Louisiana, Arkansas, and Tennessee.
The North-Western,—Kentucky, Missouri, Illinois, Indiana, Ohio, Michigan, and Territories of Wiskonsin and Iowa.

Approximate Statement of the Population, nominal Banking Capital, and Debts of the several States, at the end of the year 1840.

	January 1840. Population.	January. 1840. Bank Capital.	Interest.	July 1841. Debts.	Taxable Property.
Maine,	501,793	4,671,500	5&6	550,000 ꜰ	
N. Hampshire,	284,574	2,939,508		None	72,560,000
Vermont,	291,948	1,325,530		None	
Massachusetts,	737,699	34,485,600	5 st.	4,290,000 ꜰ	208,360,000
Rhode Island,	108,830	9,880,500		None	32,640,000
Connecticut,	310,015	8,832,223		None	97,120,000
New York,	2,428,921	52,028,793 a	5	21,000,000 d	641,360,000 g
New Jersey,	373,306	4,822,607		None	
Pennsylvania,	1,724,022	59,286,405 b	5	38,350,000 e	400,000,000 g
Delaware,	78,085	1,071,318		None	
Maryland,	469,232	10,571,630	5&6	11,490,000 ꜰ	100,000,000 g
Dist. of Colum.	43,712	1,768,074		None	
Virginia,	1,239,797	8,471,856	5&6	6,320,000 ꜰ	206,900,000 g
N. Carolina,	753,110	3,100,750		None	
S. Carolina,	594,398	11,584,355	5&6 st.	5,560,000 ꜰ	200,000,000
Georgia,	689,690	15,119,219		Not known	
Florida,	54,307	4,619,836		Not known	
Alabama,	600,000*	11,996,232	5 st.	11,500,000	
Mississippi,	375,651	30,379,403 c	5 st.	7,000,000	
Louisiana,	351,176	41,736,768	5 st.	23,730,000 ꜰ	
Arkansas,	95,642	1,951,888	5&6	3,000,000 ꜰ	
Tennessee,	829,210	7,687,556	6	7,150,000 ꜰ	121,000,000 g
Kentucky,	785,000*	8,939,003	5	3,790,000	272,000,000
Missouri,	381,102	1,116,123	5	2,500,000 ꜰ	
Illinois,	474,404	5,423,185	6 st.	12,210,000	
Indiana,	683,314	2,595,221	5	11,890,000 ꜰ	97,000,000
Ohio,	1,510,467	10,507,521	6	12,940,000 f	126,000,000
Michigan,	211,705	1,229,200	6	5,340,000 ꜰ	
Wiskonsin,	30,752	200,000		None	
Iowa,	43,068	100,000		None	
Total,	17,063,830	358,441,804		188,610,000	

* Partly on estimate.   c Great part of this annihilated.

a Including 15,227,321 free banks, half of which nominal.

b Including 35,000,000 U. S. Bank, two-thirds of which destroyed.

d Debt proper, deducting 2,054,000—Old debt provided for,.......... $13,320,000
                 Issued to Companies............ 2,845,000
                 In part of authorised do. est'd. 1,830,000
                 Loan authorised last session.. 3,000,000
                                     21,000,000

e Mr. Reed estimates interest on old 5 per cents. at 1,762,500, making Principal 35,250,000—Loan authorised last session, 3,100,000—Total, $38,350,000.

f May be increased two or three millions for completing the works; but the tolls and taxes are sufficient to pay the interest.

g In all these States the taxable property is assessed less than its value.

ꜰ All the amounts thus designated are taken from Mr. Flagg's statement.

st. The debts thus designated are, in part or wholly, payable, interest and princi-pal, at 4s. 6d. st. per dollar, or at 9½ per cent. above their nominal value. Thus the State of Mississippi will have to pay in London £1,575,000 sterling, equal to $7,665,000 for the 7,000,000 which it has received.

CPSIA information can be obtained at www.ICGtesting.com
Printed in the USA
LVOW122114290512

283777LV00012B/103/P

9 781277 975680